You're Never Upset
For the Reason
You Think

The CURE for the Common Upset

Praise for
You're Never Upset for the Reason You Think: The CURE for the Common Upset

Evolutionary Ways of Relating:

"No matter where you are in your relationships, Paul and Layne can take you to the next level and beyond. They are profound teachers of love and wisdom whose insightful distinctions reveal evolutionary ways of relating."

—**Debbie Ford,** Best-Selling Author of *The Dark Side of the Light Chasers*
and *Spiritual Divorce*

The Einsteins of Emotional Recovery:

"Layne and Paul Cutright are the Einsteins in the process and practice of conscious evolution and emotional recovery. They chart a precise course to curing within ourselves the 'common upset,' which in fact ruins our lives. They guide us skillfully in releasing any possible type of upset and moving on with our journey to realize our full potential selves."

—**Barbara Marx Hubbard,** Author of *Conscious Evolution* and *Emergence*

Giant Hearts, Gentle Humility:

"Paul and Layne's new book is a rare blend of inspiration and practicality. It helps us see all we can be, and it provides the necessary tools to get there. I love their directness, clarity, depth of caring, and incredible range of insight. They've brought together so many streams of consciousness development that it's virtually impossible not to grow with their guidance. Through it all, we can feel their giant hearts, wide open, and relax into the gentle humility of their approach. There's not a moment, person, or difficult situation that can't be uplifted by the CURE. This book belongs on the super-short list of indispensable transformational resources."

—**Raphael Cushnir,** Author of *Setting Your Heart on Fire*
and *Unconditional Bliss*

Simple Principles Into Practice:

"Here is great, great wisdom offered in an extremely reader-friendly, practical way. If more people accepted responsibility for healing their upsets, oh, what a different world this would be! Putting these simple principles into practice will bring many people closer to the happiness we all desire."

—**Alan Cohen,** Author of *I Had It All the Time*

The Secret to Resolving Emotional Conflict:

"Paul and Layne have magnificently perfected a masterpiece with this timeless wisdom. Devour every carefully crafted syllable in this book, and you'll uncover the secret to resolving emotional conflict with ease and harmony."

—**Peggy McColl,** Author of *On Being a Dog With a Bone*

New, Incredible Possibilities:

"I came to Paul and Layne in the midst of a failing marriage, but my work has gone much beyond my relationship. I have gained such clarity and distinction on not only my relationship with my wife but also my relationship with myself. I have learned how to let go of that which is not working and to focus on what I can offer to myself and to the world. In the past year, each significant relationship in my personal and professional life has seen major improvement. I feel like my heart and eyes have not only opened up to new possibilities but moved toward making new, incredible possibilities a reality!"

—**Scott Blanchard**, CEO of Coaching.com

Looking in Instead of Lashing Out:

"This book is packed with good ideas about how to get past those challenging interpersonal conflicts that we all face from time to time. The CURE is effective on many levels. It takes the steam out of an argument by forcing you to take time out to reflect on a series of questions and provides valuable tools that result in looking in instead of lashing out."

—**Elizabeth L. Allen,** Attorney and Mediator, Coast to Coast Mediation Center

A Must for Singles:

"The CURE is a powerful tool for helping transform disappointment and despair into self-knowledge and confidence. This book is a must for singles who want to enjoy the often challenging journey of finding their Life Partner and developing a fulfilling relationship."

—**David Steele,** Author of *Conscious Dating* and Founder of the Relationship Coaching Institute

Profound and Elegant Wisdom:

"We've been waiting for this book! Personal responsibility is often recommended on our website, but many find the concept hard to grasp, much less put into practice. The Cutrights clearly explain the meaning and value of taking personal responsibility, and they provide us with a road map for achieving it! The profound and elegant wisdom of this inspiring book is something we can enthusiastically recommend to everyone, confident it has the power to improve lives. Thank you, Layne and Paul!"

—**William Van Vechten,** Publisher of ConsciousLoving.com

A Knack for Simplifying the Complex:

"What a beautiful book, and such exquisite wisdom. The Cutrights have a knack for simplifying the complex, and what is more complex than human emotions? They provide a truly enlightened means to get to 'the bottom line'—which, of course, is always 'fear' and 'ego,' just particularized to each of our individual pasts and self-created neurological makeups. But how beautifully they allow a person to discover that for themselves, and to move into the higher realms of oneness and love."

—**Dr. Michael Norwood,** Author of *The Nine Insights of the Wealthy Soul*

Wonderful Book:

"This wonderful book will help you bounce back from life's difficult moments in record time and keep your eyes on the prize and your heart in the right place."

—**Robert G. Allen,** Author of *New York Times* Bestsellers *Multiple Streams of Income, Nothing Down,* and *Creating Wealth*

You're Never Upset For the Reason You Think

The CURE for the Common Upset

Layne and Paul Cutright

HEART TO HEART INTERNATIONAL
LAS VEGAS, NEVADA

You're Never Upset for the Reason You Think:
The CURE for the Common Upset

Also available as an e-book from
www.EnlightenedPartners.com

Heart to Heart International
P.O. Box 27740
Las Vegas, Nevada 89126
(702) 340-0710

ISBN: 0-9651371-1-2

Edited and produced by Just Write Literary & Editorial Partners,
www.JustWriteNow.com

ALSO BY LAYNE AND PAUL CUTRIGHT:

Straight From the Heart:
An Essential Guide for Developing, Deepening, and
Renewing Your Relationships

To contact the authors with feedback and stories of success,
e-mail Paul and Layne at
partners@EnlightenedPartners.com.

For the peacemakers of this world,
great and small, known and unknown

Contents

Preface

In 1976, we shared a mystical experience that launched our experiment in radical personal responsibility. This mystical moment came unexpectedly and unbidden.

We were colleagues working in the same office. And one day in the midst of our everyday chores, it happened. It began with a casual glance when a magic "switch" turned on some kind of tractor beam between our hearts. As we were locked in this connection, we both felt lifted into another sphere of awareness that pulsated with a rarified love neither of us had ever known before. In that moment, it felt as if our souls recognized one another and we were destined to share our lives together. Just as suddenly, the "switch" turned off, and we dropped back into normal awareness.

That experience was like a preview of coming attractions for us. We didn't want that feeling of love and connection to become just a memory: We wanted it to be an ongoing, shared reality. We had had a taste of an extraordinary awareness, and we wanted more. We were both gripped by a compelling urge to do whatever it took to get back there and stay there.

Our search led us to explore the obstacles to love in all their myriad forms. We discovered some of the universal principles about the nature of fear and the lies we tell ourselves. We discovered that assuming responsibility for our own feelings and telling the truth was a path back to this transcendent love. This path was a series of questions that worked unfailingly to return us to a higher truth where the light of understanding, trust, and compassion shone with uncommon brilliance.

We have been romantic and teaching partners for twenty-seven years now. We teach how to use relationships of all kinds as a path of personal healing and spiritual awakening. We are about to share with you some of the most important things we have learned about resolving conflict in an enlightened way. It is our deepest wish that what you learn here proves useful to you in letting go of unnecessary suffering and keeping you on a path of expanding love and wisdom.

Introduction

You get irritated in the long line at the movies, but it's not really about the people in front of you; after all, you don't even know them.

You exchange harsh words with your spouse about the grocery bill, yet underneath the argument lies something more significant than the cost of premium vitamins and gourmet potato chips.

You find yourself in an upheaval at work when someone you know is let go—and although you feel pity for your co-worker, there's a deeper, more personal anxiety nagging at you.

Opportunities for emotional turmoil abound in your life. You ignore many, while others seem to grab hold and refuse to let go. Why do some things upset you and others don't? Learning the root causes of your emotions begins with a simple understanding: *You are never upset for the reason you think.*

"Great," you may say to yourself. "If I'm never upset for the reason I think, then why am I upset?" Excellent question. If you never find out what actually upsets you, all you can do is fuss and fume and try to come up with solutions for what you guess might be the real problem.

Herein lies the power of the CURE, the Conscious Upset Resolution Exercise.

It is a new and evolutionary way of resolving your upsets and understanding yourself and your soul. With this simple, direct, personal inquiry, you can find the deeper truth, hidden beneath the seemingly obvious reasons, for any disagreement, conflict, calamity, discomfort, frustration, anguish, or emotional distress you have ever had or ever will have.

Why It's Important to Know the Real Reason

The biggest problem with believing you are upset about one thing when you're actually seething about something else is that you focus all your problem-solving in the wrong direction. If you think you are upset about the grocery bill and you create solutions for containing food expenses, it won't really calm the underlying angst if it's actually rooted in a more general fear of, say, never being able to have what you want in life. In other words, if you believe you are dealing with Problem X and are therefore applying a solution to X, it won't help if you are truly upset about Problem Y.

What's more, not knowing what you are really upset about can make a bad situation worse. Have you ever seen anyone going off half-cocked about an issue, talking to others to gain agreement, stirring up a whole lot of fear or anger only to find they were dead wrong? You may have done it yourself a few times.

When you develop the skill to look deeper than the obvious and develop solutions for the real problems, you will be able to cure the source of your problems, not just patch them up temporarily.

Look deeper than the obvious, and develop solutions for the real problems.

What you are about to learn in this book can transform your experience of arguments and upsets in your relationships. Rather than avoiding confrontation and walking on eggshells, you will be able to safely and constructively talk about things that are usually hard to discuss. You will be able to get to the other side of difficult situations in record time. Instead of misunderstandings leading to hurt feelings, resentment, and alienation, you will be able to quickly get to the heart of the problem and resolve it.

Upsets that used to last for days and weeks, or longer, will now last for only minutes or hours. Blame and resentment can now be transformed into personal power and compassion. You can acquire the skill to turn any upset into an opportunity for self-mastery. (Yes, *any* upset: Any time you are feeling less than calm, clear or serene, it would be accurate to describe yourself as "upset," which is defined as being distressed or mentally/emotionally perturbed. So the CURE will help you with everything from mild disappointment to vehement rage.)

The CURE has two parts. Part One requires "inner work" and is done alone. Part Two is "outer work" and includes a dialogue between you and the person with whom you had the upset. Detailed instructions for each part begin on page 45, but we suggest you read the entire book before you begin using the CURE for a specific upset.

The CURE, Part One: Solo Inquiry

The first step is to help you understand your part in any upset, which alone usually provides significant relief. This is because **most upsets are *internal conflicts* played out in the *external dynamics* of relationships.**

Part One consists of thirteen questions that walk you through the upset and your reaction to it, so you can find resolution and peace within yourself. The solo inquiry is useful for any kind of upset, whether it involves other people or not. You can use it to resolve negative feelings toward institutions, circumstances, or distant events over which you have no control but that are nonetheless upsetting to you.

For example, sometimes when you listen to the news, you can feel disturbed by what you hear. The CURE can provide almost instant relief for any feelings of helplessness or impotence. There will be

something you *can* do. The CURE can also be used when you feel
frustrated with inanimate objects, such as when your computer is
acting up, or your checkbook isn't balancing, or you get a flat tire.

And, of course, the CURE is invaluable in dealing with upsets
involving another person, whether a loved one, a colleague, a co-
worker, or a stranger.

The worksheet included in the back of your book walks you
through the thirteen questions of Part One. Think of it as training
wheels for a new way of thinking. In time, you will outgrow the
worksheet, and as you integrate the process, it will become second
nature to solve problems in this new way.

You will see, as you go through the solo inquiry with the
intention of finding out what you are really upset about, that you gain
an enormous amount of personal clarity. So much of what you see
and experience within yourself and the world around you depends
upon the beliefs you have internalized. Those beliefs are often hidden
from your view. The CURE enables you to observe the thoughts,
beliefs, feelings, and attitudes that have resulted in your being upset.

The CURE, Part Two: Dialogue

Part Two involves conversation with another person. With the
insights gained from Part One, you will have a whole different
perspective on what the solution to your problem might be. Some of
the resolution can happen without participation from anyone else.
But, if you do need to include someone, you will be able to
communicate from a new place that can turn the most difficult
exchange into a resounding success.

Because of your awareness of your own part in the upset, there
will be a diminished impulse to lay blame. The absence of blame in

the dialogue promotes affinity. When you have affinity with another, it is much easier to think together and understand someone else's point of view. This is the ground from which you can forge understanding and respect and create mutually beneficial outcomes.

One of the most important things to understand about upsets is they are normal, especially in relationships. Not only are they normal, but they are also predictable, inevitable, and recurring. That is, they will happen, and they will happen over and over again. As you learn how to resolve them by applying the CURE, you will notice they happen less frequently and with less intensity, even with people who are less able to take responsibility for their own issues or who don't even know about the CURE.

Seeing Upsets as Learning Opportunities

If you adopt the point of view that says life on earth is like a school, then you accept that you are here to learn lessons. Your life is your curriculum, custom designed just for you. The hard part of this, of course, is trying to figure out what it is you're supposed to be learning! The CURE will provide some signposts along the way.

If you're committed to getting these lessons instead of just getting over it, then you must recognize how shutting down and creating emotional distance in the relationship, suppressing your feelings, or pretending you aren't upset at all would be counterproductive. Driving feelings underground serves only to establish negative emotional patterns that surface in other relationships.

Instead, use upsets as opportunities to learn something new about yourself. You'll learn the true nature of the source of the problem, not just the surface appearance. When you solve the real problem, you get lasting results. If all you do is remedy a symptom, the problems keep coming back.

Most likely, they come back in the context of your relationship with someone else. You may think of your friendships, romances, family relationships, and even business associations as classrooms designed by your soul in which some of the learning opportunities are disguised as upsets. (It's been said that if life is like school, then relationships form the university.)

Upsets always contain the gift of learning, except most people have never learned how to unwrap the package. The purpose of this book is to help you do just that: unwrap the gift inherent in every upset you have ever had, or ever will have, so that you can extract the greatest possible value, thus propelling you on your path of personal and spiritual development.

CHAPTER ONE

Radical Personal Responsibility

An insult is a boon to a sage.
LAO TZU

"

My girlfriend Janet was telling me about her friendship with a new guy at work. She was talking about a conversation they'd had at lunch, and it came out that she has lunch with him a couple of times a week. As soon as I heard that, something happened in me. I got hot and kind of sweaty, and it was hard to listen to her. I just wanted to get away. I sat there for a while pretending to listen to her.

We went to the movies as we'd planned, but I wasn't really there. My mind filled with questions I was afraid to ask. Janet is pretty tuned in, and she could tell I wasn't myself. She kept asking if I was okay. I kept saying everything was fine. Well, I'm not a great liar, and I kind of wanted to talk about it anyway. I just wanted her to open me up.

We went to a coffee shop and I started to talk. I told her I didn't like hearing about this guy at work, and I was probably jealous. Janet is great. She listened to me and was real sweet, reaching out across the table to touch my hand. I felt pretty stupid.

We had been using the CURE for about a year, and she suggested that she lead me through the process right there in the restaurant. Because I had some practice with the CURE, it was pretty straightforward finding out what my bottom-line thought was. It came from an issue that I was already aware of and hadn't totally handled yet. I remember wondering if I was ever going to get over it. Fear of loss. Fear of loss. God, how I hate that feeling!

The hard part for me, still, is knowing what to do about it. I know it is a big improvement for me to be able to see the real problem. I can easily remember a time when I would have just broken up with Janet to get the pain over with. At least I don't do that anymore. But healing my heart seems to be another story.

If I am really honest with myself, I can see I haven't really applied myself to this "fear of loss" thing. I've been avoiding it. But I can see now that if I don't handle it, my relationship with Janet will never be what I really want it to be. I'll just keep finding ways of pushing her away because I'm afraid of losing her. It sounds crazy, but that's what I do. I never knew that before using the CURE.

Since the problem seems too big to handle on my own, I've decided to get a relationship coach who knows more than I do. There is also a practice group for the CURE that Janet and I used to go to. I think we should start going again. I think I just have to be determined to put this problem behind me and heal it once and for all. I am tired of living with it. I believe I can do it, and I just have to get the support.

        ”

Jealousy and other emotions like it can appear to be happening to us or to be inflicted on us by others. But to address the root cause of any upset, you must learn to observe the internal factors that shape your own perceptions and reactions. We call this ability to observe yourself and realize your power to alter these perceptions and reactions *radical personal responsibility.*

We call it radical because it is such a departure from what is commonly thought of as responsibility, which can mean laying blame. Instead, it is insight into the deeper workings of your mind that illuminates how you have contributed to any challenging situation before you.

When you take personal responsibility, what are you taking responsibility for? You are taking responsibility for your own consciousness and the effects it creates. The thoughts, beliefs, feelings, attitudes, impressions, perceptions, and interpretations—all of which you hold in your consciousness—can be a matter of choice. If you are like most people, you are unaware of all the moments of choosing that go into your beliefs and your interpretations. You probably haven't noticed you are making choices all the time, choices that determine the possibilities that will be open or closed to you in your future.

If it feels as if your beliefs just show up fully developed and you have nothing to do with how they came to be a part of you, it is because you have not developed the ability to observe your own mind. The CURE will help you.

Most of your beliefs were probably "absorbed" from your family when you were younger. The rest of them were gleaned from the community you grew up in and from the culture at large. The process of acquiring them was invisible to you, so you didn't notice you were doing it. It happened silently, in the background of your life.

Uncovering that awareness and accepting personal responsibility is an acquired skill. If it wasn't demonstrated for you when you were growing up, or you haven't intentionally studied it, chances are you haven't a clue about how to do it. A start is to recognize what personal responsibility is not. In the absence of personal responsibility, all you can do is blame others for your difficulties because it looks to you as if they *are* to blame. This forever dooms you to a "victim" mentality that separates you from your personal power and spiritual and relational maturity. The CURE will teach you, step by step, to approach life's hurdles in a different way that both enlightens and empowers you.

Once you learn to practice radical personal responsibility, you will find a source of inner strength and power that no one can ever take away from you. Because of your ability to take authentic, empowered responsibility, you will find that, in time, upsets become less frequent, of shorter duration, and less intense. This means you have more time and energy to focus on living the kind of life and sharing the kind of relationships you truly want and deserve.

New peace, harmony, and power fill your relationships when you practice radical personal responsibility. Through it, you enter a more refined sphere of relating that enhances your life and accelerates the realization of your ultimate spiritual self. Practicing radical personal responsibility forever changes the way you approach and resolve conflict.

When you assume radical personal responsibility, you live in a truth that proclaims,

I am responsible for how I allow others to affect me.

*In a world of forces beyond my control, I can learn to be
the keeper of my own heart and mind.*

*Even when things appear not to be going my way,
and I am upon an emotional sea
of crossing and diverging currents,
I can still navigate my way to my ultimate good fortune.*

I proclaim that I am not a victim of the world I see.

I am a co-creator of it.

*Let love and wisdom be my moral compass,
and let clarity be the wind in my sails.*

All Beliefs Are Not Created Equal

Radical personal responsibility is the ability to observe your own mind and make conscious choices about what thoughts, feelings, and interpretations you will continue to maintain. Part of becoming a mature adult is developing your ability to be more aware of this process and taking more control of it. It begins with the ability to observe and reflect on your own thinking.

Rather than just having thoughts, you start to examine why you think what you think. You start to notice there are other ways to think about the same things, and you start to choose the kind of thinking that will serve you best. You can be responsible for your consciousness by being more discriminating about the beliefs you hold, the feelings you focus on, and the values you embrace.

Dr. Milton Rokeach, a renowned psychologist, distinguished five kinds of beliefs.

1. **Basic beliefs** are socially shared; e.g., "We all need to eat in order to live." These kinds of beliefs tend to be facts about our universal experience as human beings.

2. **Personal beliefs** are not socially shared; e.g., "I can never do anything right," or "I am God's gift to women." These beliefs are concerned with self-identity and your view of the world and are completely subjective. These kinds of beliefs are assessments and may or may not have anything to do with reality.

3. **Authority beliefs** are those outside our direct experience. They result from others whose

authority we assess as credible; e.g., "CNN is the most accurate news network."

4. **Derived beliefs** are a variation of authority beliefs in that they rely on identification with the authority. This is how we acquire beliefs from our culture, religion, and our family; e.g., "Suicide attacks on our enemies are justified because martyrdom is good, and we have no other means of defense."

5. **Inconsequential beliefs** are simply a matter of preference and personal taste; e.g., "Steve Martin is a funnier comedian than Billy Crystal." They are opinions.

Your consciousness is a powerful force for creating. It determines the people you are attracted to and the people who are attracted to you. If you want to improve your lot in life or the quality of your relationships, choosing to accept personal responsibility is the first and most important step. It allows you to address negative beliefs in numbers 2, 3, and 4 above: personal beliefs that determine self-identity and world view, authority beliefs that we accept from others we see as more informed, and derived beliefs from authorities with whom we are identified.

Who's Really Responsible?

Often it looks as if we get upset because people aren't doing what we want them to do or what we think they should do. It looks as if we are upset because of something other than ourselves.

We are asserting that **your upset is caused by something inside of you rather than something external to you.** Any pain you feel already existed within you as a pool of negative thoughts and feelings formed in your past and is merely triggered by another person or event.

In other words, most upsets are an activation of unresolved pain from your past. It is one thing to know about this idea and quite another to practice it. And that is exactly what the CURE is all about. Personal responsibility goes beyond simply saying you are responsible. It is a set of actions you take that begins with self-reflection.

Assuming personal responsibility means accepting a new mantle of power, and it has a price: The price is letting go of thinking and speaking like a victim.

Most upsets are an activation of unresolved pain from your past.

Even though you may have been victimized, you have begun to realize that thinking like a victim can only make a bad situation worse. When you step outside of the victim mentality, you cross the threshold into a new world of personal power. You can surrender the illusion that anyone other than you has power or authority over your life. Stephen Covey wrote, "Our ultimate freedom is the right and power to decide how anybody or anything outside ourselves will affect us."

Radical personal responsibility means you no longer get to indulge your tendency to blame others for your feelings, reactions, interpretations, or choices. Through the art of personal responsibility you will be lifted above the illusion that any upset is something that has happened *to* you. You will see that unwittingly you have contributed to the situation you find yourself in. When you discover how and why you did that, you can create lasting change, so that this kind of thing doesn't keep happening in your life over and over and over again.

Personal responsibility indicates mature self-love. When you love yourself, you want to give yourself the best chance to succeed. The art of radical personal responsibility is to know what it is *within you* that contributed to the upset and then to follow through on your insights and make the internal changes that are appropriate.

Through the years, you have probably noticed that being passive about happiness is not always effective. Often you have to reach into life to have what you want. If you know that your beliefs can affect your focus and choices, doesn't it make sense to ensure your beliefs are of the highest quality possible?

"

I came home from work tired, looking forward to a nice meal and a relaxing evening. As I opened the door, I could hear my eleven-year-old Mat screaming at his younger sister, Sarah, age nine.

Something sparked in me, and I went into a mindless rage. I stormed into the living room and yanked Mat into his room. I barely remember what I was screaming at him.

I went into my own room and sat on the bed feeling tired, defeated, and very bad about myself. As I glanced at my bedside table, I remembered I had a stash of blank CURE worksheets in the drawer. The process had been so helpful many times before, and I felt my spirits lift a little bit knowing there was something I could do to feel better.

After I went in to check on Sarah, I sat down with the CURE, pen in hand. About twenty minutes later, I came out of my room feeling like a different person. The most helpful part of the exercise was finding my "bottom-line thought" and understanding why I had reacted so strongly.

Then I did some "energy tapping" on some of the old childhood family stuff that the CURE revealed, and I felt immediately better. After my head cleared, I knew what I needed to do to remedy the situation for my kids and me.

I was able to apologize to Mat, and we had a good cry together. We all helped cook dinner, and afterward we all sat down as a family to talk about what had happened. I am so glad I had done my inner work so I could guide the conversation with Mat and Sarah. I had pretty much gotten though my own issue so I could help them talk through their different versions of "the story."

When I was younger, my dad was always yelling at my brothers. Sometimes the anger filled our house, and there was no way to get away from it. I felt trapped and helpless and angry, but there wasn't anything I could do about it. That is what had gotten triggered when I walked through the door that night.

My eyes kept tearing up as my kids listened to me. Their faces were so sweet and open. I so much wanted to protect them from the pain of angry words and violent feelings. I talked to them about how hurtful words can stay deep inside and keep hurting people for a long, long time. I said I was deeply sorry for any time I had been hurtful with them in the past and I wanted all of us to do better in the future. We felt close to one another as we were talking about all of it. I could tell Mat was taking extra care to be a good big brother with Sarah as they were getting ready for bed.

As I was going to sleep that night I kept thinking about how it felt growing up in a house full of anger and how much I didn't want that in my life anymore. I didn't want it for me, and I didn't want it for my kids. It felt like some kind of family disease that was getting passed down from generation to generation.

When I look back on that night, I see it as a turning point for my family and me. We got some books on anger and went to a family therapist. There was a lot about handling anger in healthy and safe ways that I had never learned. Together we learned to deal with our feelings better. We all know how to use the CURE, and it is just a part of how we work out our problems. It feels so much better to truly understand why I get upset and to be able to think clearly and find new solutions.

〝〝

How Science Supports Radical Personal Responsibility

In the mid-1960s, two neurobiologists at the University of Chile, Humberto Maturana and Francisco Varela, began to explore and redefine human cognition. Their classic book, *The Tree of Knowledge: The Biological Roots of Human Understanding,* proposes a revolutionary way of looking at the world through the lens of self-determination. Simply said, **your experience of the world is determined by you, not the world.**

They inspire this example: If you shoot an arrow at a tree and another arrow at a deer, the difference in the impact on the two is less a consequence of the arrow and more a result of the two targets' different structures.

The structure of a tree is roots, bark, trunk, branches, and foliage. The structure of a deer is flesh, blood, bones, nervous system, organs, and hide. An arrow piercing the bark of a tree has little or no impact on the tree's vitality. An arrow piercing the hide of a deer can puncture vital organs with a subsequent loss of life. Same arrow, different structures, different results.

Now, imagine seeing a tree, a deer, and a person standing side by side. Along comes another person. He stops and turns to the three of them and says, "I don't like you. You are ugly." The effect his words have on the tree and the deer are insignificant. The deer may react to the sound or voice tone, but the words themselves would have no effect. The effect those same words might have on the human being could be quite dramatic. Same stimulus, different structures, different results.

When you receive different stimuli from your environment, for example, someone gives you a disapproving look or someone accuses you of being selfish or fails to keep an agreement with you or you get some bad news, these are all just like the arrow. How these things affect you depends on your *psychological structure*.

The Complex Psyche of a Human Being

We are biological, psychological, and spiritual beings. At the physical level we all appear to share similar characteristics: skin, skeleton, blood, nerves, etc. And in this very predictable aspect of our structure we do find delightful variety. But who we are as human beings goes far beyond anything that can be seen.

The first of these unseen aspects is psychological, which is the storehouse of our beliefs. Beliefs are complex thought systems that carry with them the compelling force of emotion. Our beliefs take root in our mental-emotional structure, which directs the interpretations we make of the world around us.

As we mentioned earlier, the beliefs that determine your interpretations are rarely examined. You are unaware of them because they dwell below the horizon of your awareness. We can refer to this invisible matrix of beliefs as the *conditioned self*.

You started being "conditioned" by your environment from the day you were born. You began having experiences, some pleasurable, some painful. You were conditioned by your instinctive impulse to search for pleasure and avoid pain. If you associate certain stimuli with pleasure, you condition a pleasurable response. If you associate specific stimuli with pain, you condition a painful or fearful response. Over time, through repetition, your responses become automatic. You don't think; you react.

Consider Pavlov's classic study of dogs. Every time a research scientist fed a dog, he rang a bell. Over time the dogs became

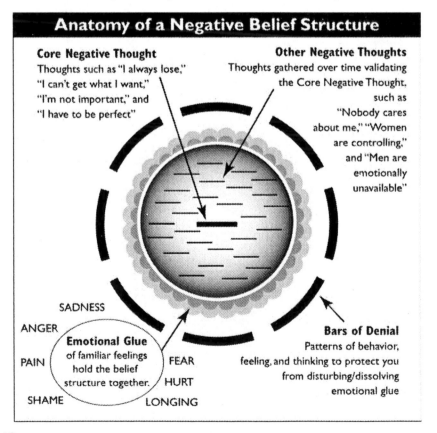

Anatomy of a Negative Belief Structure

Core Negative Thought
Thoughts such as "I always lose," "I can't get what I want," "I'm not important," and "I have to be perfect"

Other Negative Thoughts
Thoughts gathered over time validating the Core Negative Thought, such as "Nobody cares about me," "Women are controlling," and "Men are emotionally unavailable"

SADNESS
ANGER
Emotional Glue
of familiar feelings hold the belief structure together.
PAIN
FEAR
HURT
SHAME
LONGING

Bars of Denial
Patterns of behavior, feeling, and thinking to protect you from disturbing/dissolving emotional glue

"conditioned" to salivate at the sound of the bell, even when there was no food present.

You were conditioned by the beliefs, emotions, fears, prejudices, moods, and behaviors of the people around you when you were growing up. You were conditioned by punishment and reward. This "conditioning" still causes you to act mindlessly in defense of your emotional and physical survival. This conditioning has become part of your "structure" and determines how you will be affected by things that happen.

The preceding diagram illustrates what a negative belief structure might look like if you could see it. It is these invisible negative belief structures that get triggered, causing you to become upset.

Personal power comes from becoming aware of your own negative belief structures, learning how they operate to create your interpretations and experience of reality and, most important, learning how to neutralize or change them so they do not cause you any more pain.

Each of Us Has a Spiritual Self

Each of us also has a spiritual aspect, a mysterious, often indiscernible part of us. Humans, spiritual beings animated in biological form, have been trying to understand the nature of spirit, or the soul, through religion and philosophy, poetry and art, since we first began to sense spirit's presence. Although the debate about the ultimate nature of spirit will continue beyond our lifetimes, from our experience we can see that universal spiritual motives are fairly well-defined:

- ◆ to evolve.

- ◆ to act out of inspired vision rather than to react only from the animal survival instinct; to overcome irrational fears.

- ◆ to see deeply into the nature of reality and respond to its complexity with wisdom and compassion.

- ◆ to know that we are all connected and to seek mutually beneficial outcomes.

To personally know the divine reality through direct experience is a noble goal and a vital one. This direct knowing goes far beyond belief, faith, or being able to talk about it. This knowledge is something so visceral, so palpable, that you can taste it. Once you have had this taste, it infuses your thoughts, feelings, motives, and actions. Your life becomes informed by this knowing.

Alas, it is rarely a permanent experience. But, once you have tasted it, it becomes the measuring stick of truth and love for every other experience you have. It becomes a moral compass for your life. And regaining this perspective again and again and again will become one of your most valued skills.

This ability will help you regain your sanity in an insane situation. It will comfort you during times of loss. It will nourish you and sustain you through times of uncertainty. It will illuminate a path when you are in uncharted territory. It can help you stand unshaken by adverse turns of events. It will guide you in becoming your best.

The Conditioned Self and the Higher Self

The structure of a human being includes both the conditioned self (psychological) and the spiritual self, often referred to as the *higher self.* When you experience what is good and true and beautiful about yourself, you are experiencing your higher self. These different psychological and spiritual structures are what determine the effect relationships with others have on you.

When you are upset with another person, you are faced with a choice: to tune in to the voice of spirit, seeking expansion and deeper understanding, or to listen to the voice of the conditioned self's desire for safety and the familiar. The higher self gets curious. The conditioned self gets defensive.

To honor the spirit is to accept the opportunity for your healing and personal evolution. When you choose to assume radical personal responsibility, knowing that you are responsible for the effect external circumstances have on you, you are taking a stand for the power of your spiritual nature to run the show.

The higher self gets curious.

Consider this example. A man innocently announces to his romantic partner that he wants to spend the weekend fishing with his buddies, and the woman gets upset. *He'd rather not spend the weekend with me, and I am unimportant to him,* she believes. Her upset is most likely the result of a triggered mental-emotional structure *within her* that interprets his choice to mean something negative about her. Her mental-emotional structure, not his choice to go fishing, causes her pain.

Another woman without that particular mental-emotional structure may very well have a completely different and positive response to her boyfriend's fishing trip. *We can each have our separate lives and interests and still feel connected,* she believes. Same

communication, different mental-emotional structure, different
result.

Creating New Results Out of Old Patterns

Upsets, disagreements, misunderstandings, miscommunications,
and breakdowns are a part of life. Everybody has them at one time or
another. Upsets can be anything from minor misunderstandings to
devastating conflicts that tear relationships apart. Sometimes upsets
can be so destructive that they cause permanent damage to
relationships. Misunderstandings can also last for years and even
generations: long enough that people forget why they are supposed to
be upset!

Almost invariably, beliefs are the source of your recurrent upsets
in relationships. Many people notice a pattern to their upsets, or that
the same kind of thing upsets them over and over again. ("Why do I
keep getting ripped off in business?" "Why can't I find a job where
they appreciate me?" "Why do I always end up with guys who ignore
me?" "Why do women always take advantage of me?" and so on.)
However, noticing recurring patterns and being able to *do something*
corrective and preventive are two different things. Practicing the
CURE allows you to resolve negative and painful relationship
patterns by clearing the source of them.

You don't have to be stuck in old ways of thinking, trapped
within the confines of old interpretations you have made or inherited
from your family or culture. You can slip away from the tyranny of
the familiar, or the mindset that prevents you from seeing each event
as a wholly new experience unrelated to *apparently* similar events.

For example, you would be able to interpret a person's conduct
without the obscuring prejudice of your previous judgments about

someone else's behavior. Not all men are the same. Not all women are the same. Not all bosses are the same. Not all people who look alike are the same.

When you can clearly see the reality of a situation, rather than your interpretations of the situation, you can make better choices. You can think more clearly. You can create a better map to get where you want to go because you know where you really are. Seeing the truth in a situation gives you real power.

CHAPTER TWO

The Ground on Which We Stand

**And we shall tame
the savageness of man
and make gentle
the life of this world.**

INSPIRED BY ROBERT KENNEDY'S ADDRESS AFTER MARTIN
LUTHER KING, JR.'S ASSASSINATION

In 1995, we were invited to present our work at the Third Annual International Conference on Conflict Resolution in St. Petersburg, Russia. There were about two hundred participants representing more than twenty countries. We had been teaching the CURE for many years and were excited about the opportunity to present our work on an international stage to such a diverse audience.

Among the many things we discovered as the conference proceeded were the blind assumptions we had about resolving conflicts that were not taken into account in our presentation. Fortunately, we were scheduled to present in the middle of the conference, so we had the opportunity to think about and distinguish these assumptions before we did our workshop. We present them here for your consideration.

For some, these assumptions will seem normal, and you will recognize, as we did, that you simply take them for granted. For others, accepting some or all of these assumptions will represent an important part of the work you must do to master the art and skill of conscious conflict resolution.

When we practice the CURE, we assume the following.

1. Humans are naturally inclined to grow and evolve.

After our essential physical needs are satisfied, we are naturally attracted to bettering ourselves in more advanced ways. Psychologist Abraham Maslow articulated a natural hierarchy of needs in all human beings. Once the needs of one level are satisfied, we give more attention to the satisfaction of the next level of need. The hierarchy of needs unfolds in the following order:

- the need for warmth, shelter and food, then

- the need for safety and security, then

- the need for connection and belonging, then

- the need for respect and status, then

- the need for self-actualization.

We all have a natural drive to evolve and to manifest our highest potential. If human beings are given the opportunity to better themselves, they usually take it. The CURE gives people a practical tool for bettering themselves.

Conscious conflict resolution promotes the satisfaction of all levels of need. It can be very difficult, but not impossible to practice when your basic physical needs are unmet. Malnutrition, chemical imbalances, and diseases of various kinds can interfere with the ability to think clearly or creatively.

2. We are equally deserving of respect and understanding.

Enlightened conflict resolution can exist only in an atmosphere of equality. We may not be equal in intelligence or experience or status, but we are equal in our right to be treated with dignity and caring. It is not assumed that one person has more privilege than another. It is not assumed that one person is entitled to more respect or understanding than another. It is not assumed that one person's feelings are more important than another's. When we use the CURE, we endeavor to keep this in mind.

3. We prefer harmony to discord.

All of our needs are more easily satisfied if we can cooperate harmoniously. It is a matter of enlightened self-interest to preserve harmony where we can.

4. Everyone involved has a willingness to resolve the differences.

We may not know how, but we are all willing to resolve the situation to our mutual satisfaction. We both see the benefit to ourselves in resolving our differences to our mutual satisfaction.

We are motivated from within to resolve this situation. We don't have to be controlled or coerced into it. In fact, we probably won't be able to find a mutually beneficial outcome unless we are all participating in a spirit of good intention. The idea is that we are going to work together to find a resolution that works for everyone.

5. Blame is toxic, destroys trust, inhibits healing, and prevents resolution.

In the absence of personal responsibility, blame seems logical. But blaming and punishing attitudes are counterproductive in conflict resolution. The sooner we can unburden ourselves of blame, the more effective we can be. Blaming others only entrenches us in the role of the victim, removing us from our highest expression of personal power.

Playing the victim can sometimes feel safe and give us a false sense of power in a peculiar way. But whatever benefit we may imagine pales in comparison to the benefit that comes from taking responsibility for the aspects of ourselves (known or unknown) that may have contributed to this difficult situation.

We want to take responsibility for ourselves without inducing or deepening our guilt and without relieving others of the opportunity of taking responsibility for their part in the upset. We all make mistakes, and learning and growing from them in a spirit of forgiveness is an essential part of enlightened conflict resolution. Through using the CURE, we can let go of blame and shift to personal responsibility, which promotes trust.

6. Love and affinity are healing agents.

Miracles can happen in a spirit of goodwill. We can be empowered to find new solutions when we are willing to answer these questions: *What would love do here? What would love say here? What is the most loving attitude I can have for myself and others in this difficult situation?*

We are not at our most resourceful when we are distracted by unpleasant feelings of contention and judgment. The sooner we can find something in the other to have affinity for, the sooner we can build a bridge of understanding.

7. If one person loses in the relationship, the whole relationship suffers.

For some people, conflict resolution can mean anything from validating their own point of view with overwhelming evidence, thus invalidating the other's point of view, to eliminating the other person altogether. You must do whatever it takes to win, thus ending the conflict! We believe this old attitude of might makes right is going the way of the dinosaurs.

One of the biggest problems with this old way of thinking is that you aren't sufficiently motivated to find a solution that can work for everyone involved. You may be willing for others to be the losers as long as you can feel like the winner.

This is very shortsighted. Winning, and thereby causing others to lose, often has undesirable consequences down the road for *you*. They may feel resentful or intimidated, or even worse, the need to retaliate. Losing with you usually means they will not bring the highest and best parts of themselves to a relationship with you.

But it is the highest and best in people that usually translates into more harmony, creativity, and synergy. If you are willing to settle for people losing around you, you usually end up creating relationships where you have to use your own valuable energy to control them.

The valuable potential of the whole relationship is lost when part of the relationship loses. This understanding has birthed a common American term called *win-win*.

8. *Relationships can be used for healing, learning, and growth.*

Your relationships are actually mirrors of your own consciousness. When you learn to see your own reflection in the quality of your relationships with others, you catapult yourself on your path of personal growth and spiritual evolution.

When you look into the mirror and see that your collar needs adjusting, do you reach out to the mirror to adjust your collar? Of course not! You use what you see in the mirror to more effectively change what you need to change on your own person.

The same principle holds true in relationships. Look into the mirror of your relationships and use the reflection to change what needs to be changed *within your own consciousness.*

It is important to resist the temptation to make other people change without first looking at what needs to be shifted within yourself. It can seem quite miraculous that as you change yourself, the reflection in the mirror of your relationships changes, too.

"
_____

My kitty, Patches, is as precious to me as any friend I've ever had. When I hear myself say that, it shocks me, but I still can't deny that it is true. She is not a haughty, uppity cat. She loves to greet me when I come home. She comes to cuddle on my lap every night at eight, regular as clockwork. She sits on my lap and purrs and looks up at me with a face so full of sweetness that I find myself sometimes lost in the wonder of her. It is a time of slowing down and feeling peace and contentment. It is often a prelude to deep reflection and meditation. It surprises me how much I enjoy my relationship with her.

I was beside myself when I came home from work to discover she had broken her leg. My husband and I rushed her to the emergency vet. After a couple of hours of waiting, X rays and a $3,500 surgery estimate, I sat on my couch trying to collect my thoughts and calm myself.

Using the CURE was helpful on many levels over the next few days. Being able to clearly see the beliefs that were causing me pain allowed me to gain a clearer perspective so I could remain decisive in an emotionally intense time.

I felt painfully conflicted. This vet bill couldn't have come at a worse time. We had recently experienced a huge financial setback. We were swimming in debt and just barely able to meet our monthly expenses. We had tightened our belts, so to speak, and weren't allowing ourselves any frivolous expenses. Being at a place in my life where I had to look at the dollar value of my beloved pet was pulling me into an emotional tailspin.

I could tell that the thought that I was helpless was triggered big time. But instead of falling into a heap of self-pity, I was able to pull myself out of it and use this painful situation to grow. I was able to look at all the options, discuss them with my husband without getting into a fight, and come to a decision that we both could feel good about. That may not sound like much to most people, but it is a dramatic improvement from the way I used to handle things, which was to get hysterical.

I think one of the most valuable things I have gotten from practicing the CURE is learning to observe my emotional reactions to things. I never used to stop and notice what I was feeling and why I was feeling that way; I just acted my feelings out. I often made a bad situation even worse with that kind of behavior. Now I am able to manage my feelings much better. Thank goodness!

There were many learning opportunities in this little catastrophe, but one of them surprised me quite a bit. After Patches came home from the vet, she was so vulnerable, in pain, and looked a mess. Her whole hind leg was shaved with a six-inch incision closed with twenty staples. They had shaved other parts of her to connect IVs and other surgical stuff. She looked like a drunken dog-groomer had mistaken her for a French poodle and passed out before he could finish the job. When I would watch her limping around trying to get comfortable, my chest would get tight, like my heart was breaking, and my breath got shallow.

But here is the surprising part: As I was unraveling my upset about my poor hurt kitty, I discovered how I was seeing myself in her. The financial setback we were working so hard to recover from had left me feeling *vulnerable and broken in a way that I hadn't recognized. I was trying to tough it out and just get through it.*

Because the CURE trained me to look deeper than the obvious and to search for the healing opportunity in every upset, I was able to use my kitty's accident as a catalyst for a deeper level of healing for myself, as well. I was able to acknowledge and tend to feelings I had been in denial of. I was able to give myself permission to heal a fragile part of myself and to give myself a share of the tenderness I could so easily give to my little friend, Patches.

This led to a deeper feeling of connection with my husband. I hadn't realized how much I was bracing myself against my inner pain in a way that was shutting him out. We talked, I cried, he held me. Somehow, in an almost miraculous way, we turned this hard time into a healing time.

〝〞

The CURE is an evolutionary approach to resolving upsets. Instead of escalating an argument into shouting, name-calling, manipulation, the "silent treatment," or capitulation, when you notice that you are having an emotional reaction to anything, you stop and ask yourself some very important questions. Instead of forging ahead on top of roiling emotional undercurrents, trying to solve the problem, you take a time-out and use the CURE and discover how the interior world of your heart and mind is being played out on the stage of players you see with your body's eyes.

The CURE illuminates the real cause of your emotional reactions and leads you to rapid insight. This heightened insight reveals solutions that will be significantly more effective than what you might have come up with before using the CURE.

The CURE teaches you the steps of personal responsibility. With *regular* application it can take you beyond the mere concept of personal responsibility to proficiency and masterful application in all domains of your life.

Personal responsibility is absolutely essential for having your relationships be the way you want them to be. It is a necessary element for high-level relationships in which you want to inspire cooperation rather than control others' behavior through fear. Co-creating solutions in complex group relationships, in which you want everyone to benefit, can happen only when each person has clarity about why they want what they want, or need what they need. Everyone must also be willing to take the initiative in creating it rather than hoping or waiting passively for it to come to pass.

Personal responsibility also determines whether you are able to manage your fears well enough to refrain from contributing to adversarial dynamics. To the mature person, personal responsibility is seen as the seat of personal power and the key to success in relationships.

The CURE is designed to help you use any upset as a platform for personal growth and spiritual evolution. The purpose of the CURE is to identify and resolve the root cause of any given upset and to transform anger, hurt, blame, and defense into understanding, compassion, trust, and cooperation. For you to achieve this, you must complete the entire exercise. Do not stop at any point just because you feel "better." To get the full benefit, you must finish all of it.

Three Aspects for Conscious Conflict Resolution

There are three aspects to consider in using upsets as an opportunity for personal growth and spiritual evolution: mental, emotional, and spiritual.

Your Mental Aspect

The mental aspect is concerned with intellectual comprehension, which is characterized by *insight*. Insight alone does not complete the job in your growth opportunity. In fact, it is usually just the beginning. You must use the insight. You must use it to make different choices so that you can create different results. Understanding why you react the way you do may be helpful, but it doesn't *automatically* transfer into greater wisdom or ability.

With the CURE, you will become the observer of your thinking process. You will explore why you think what you think. Often, when you want to make changes in your life, you must reflect on your thinking. Your thoughts become beliefs that become feelings that become attitudes that determine the choices you make. Your choices determine the results in your life. If you want to change the results you are getting, you have to look at your beliefs.

You will become the observer of your thinking process.

Beliefs are a mighty force in your relationships. When things aren't going well, one of the first things you want to consider is, "What beliefs could create this reality?" The next logical step is to change the limiting beliefs—to do something with the insight. We will be exploring in chapter 5 different techniques you can use to change your limited thinking and your beliefs, if a change is what you want.

Your Emotional Aspect

The second aspect in conscious conflict resolution is concerned with clarity of feelings, characterized by the ability to *identify* them as well as *express* them in safe and appropriate ways. Exploring feelings and learning how to honor them doesn't seem to come easily for many people. It is a learned skill for most.

Just talking about your vulnerable feelings can seem like an enormous risk. Learning how to talk about your feelings and to listen to other people talk about theirs, without reacting in a negative way, is one of the most important social skills you can learn.

When you can't talk about your feelings directly, they tend to leak into your relationships in undesirable ways. The feelings you can't acknowledge, and thereby relieve, are driven underground and then tend to erupt seemingly out of nowhere later. Sometimes they recur in the same relationship, but they can even bleed through to other relationships.

Feelings triggered at work can determine your voice tone and body language with your family, for example. Feelings have enormous power to impact every aspect of our lives; they are not easily compartmentalized. Feelings dictate your willingness or unwillingness to ask for what you want and your ability to inspire cooperation or turn people off. Feelings can determine the possibilities that you see are available to you and whether you notice and take advantage of opportunities or let them pass you by.

Feelings have enormous power to impact every aspect of our lives.

Most people don't know why they feel the way they do. Do your feelings influence your behavior without you knowing it? Have you ever gotten your feelings hurt and then said something nasty without even thinking about it? Have you ever gotten so angry that you completely stopped speaking to someone forever, without ever checking to see if you had the facts straight? Have you ever failed to pursue an opportunity because you felt uncertain about yourself? When you act blindly out of your feelings, you can limit and even damage your relationships. You can do things you will regret, hurt others, or embarrass yourself and even hold yourself back from expressing your highest potential.

But your feelings can be your greatest teachers *if you will listen to them*. Paying attention to your feelings is necessary if you want to be a whole and healthy person. Listening to your feelings doesn't mean you will always do what they tell you to do. But listening and learning from your feelings will help you understand why you are feeling the way you are, and this is essential for making new and different choices. Making wise choices is necessary to resolving conflicts in an effective way.

Just as you are never upset for the reason you think, it is just as true to say that **you aren't feeling what you're feeling because of the reason you think**. Here is where one of the most powerful learning opportunities in the CURE comes through.

Your Spiritual Aspect

There is a higher part of you that knows what unresolved emotional dynamics from your past are weakening you. These unresolved issues interfere with your ability to realize your highest potential. Simply put, your unresolved emotional issues drain your personal power and your ability to feel ongoing joy and peace. It becomes essential for these hidden issues to come to the surface of your awareness. Then you can sort them out and resolve them from the higher level of wisdom you have gained since they occurred originally. Upsets are methods your higher self has of pointing out your unfinished business from the past, so that you can unburden yourself and move lightly down the path of your own personal adventure.

If you pay attention to the emotional triggers in an upset, you can use the information to take back your power from these silent, invisible forces that cheat you of your highest potential. As you pay attention, you discover that most of your negative feelings are simply a replay of unfinished business from the past.

The upset is not a bad thing; it is a hidden healing opportunity. You may think you are feeling lonely because your girlfriend cancelled a date, but as you look deeper, you see that this loneliness comes from all those years you were left alone after school without a caregiver. When you resolve this old issue, you can find new ways of dealing with and even enjoying solitude.

It may look to you as if you are upset because someone who is supposed to be your friend has been gossiping about you. But as you look deeper, you see that what has been triggered is a well of mistrust that was created from feeling betrayed by your brother when you were young. When you gain perspective on this old hurt, you can make new choices about your friendships today.

You may feel you have to lie to protect yourself when it is discovered you have made a mistake at work. But as you look deeper, you see an old memory has been triggered when you were humiliated in class. This memory has all the emotional potency of the original event when your fourth grade teacher chastised you for giving the wrong answer. This memory is broadcasting in your body right now as if the past was being replayed in the present. When you acknowledge the beliefs that were built on this unhealed pain, you create a new mental-emotional structure that provides safety even when you are not perfect.

As you see these kinds of things in yourself, you can use the awareness to further heal and finally complete these old issues, thereby freeing yourself from recycling them over and over in your important relationships and with other people and organizations.

"

When my thirteen-year-old son, Jason, was dismissed from his school wrestling team, he was surprised and devastated. When I asked him what happened, he said he didn't know and he hadn't seen it coming. He was clearly confused and hurt. I have had great success in using the CURE for myself, and my wife and I have also used it together for our relationship. So I thought I would try it with Jason and see if I could help him sort out this problem.

With a little probing using the line of questioning in the CURE, I learned that he was dissatisfied with being given only exhibition matches to wrestle in. He wanted to be on the team and thought he was good enough to wrestle in "matches that counted." Then he revealed that he told his coach that if he couldn't be in real matches, he was going to quit the team. The coach said, fine, if that's what he wanted to do. Not the response Jason had been expecting!

Jason had thought his coach would encourage him to stay on the team and give him an idea when he would be ready to move beyond exhibition matches. With the CURE, we learned that Jason's false bravado in threatening to quit was masking his underlying uncertainty about his ability. He wanted the coach to reassure him and encourage him, and thought that was what the coach would do. When that didn't happen, his bottom-line thought, I'm not good enough, got triggered with very intense feelings of low self-esteem and a sinking feeling.

I was able to help Jason see that it wasn't the coach who was making him feel that way, but that he was already dealing with the thought of not being good enough in a lot of areas of his life right now. He was starting to be interested in girls, he was developing new friendships in his new middle school and was being challenged academically, so there were lots of opportunities to feel "not good enough." The coach's comment was just the event that brought it all to the surface. Understandably, he wanted to lash out at the coach.

Jason was able to see that his ploy to get the coach's approval was not the best way to go about getting what he wanted. He could see that it would have been much better for him to be straight with his coach and ask what it was going to take for him to be ready to wrestle in "real matches." Granted, the coach could have handled it differently, and I think there are some more conversations to be had about Jason's performance and getting back on the team. But the important thing is that the CURE helped Jason learn a valuable lesson about himself.

As much as is possible with a thirteen-year-old, I think Jason is seeing this situation as a learning opportunity. And I am grateful I can help him not be so hard on himself.

"

Seize the Healing Opportunity

You learn to seize the healing opportunity by paying attention to your feelings, discovering where they are coming from, getting mad or sad about what you are *really* feeling mad or sad about, and then letting the emotional energy move through and out of you without judging it.

This emotional purge is what you need to move on. Then you bring in the higher wisdom you have gained through your adult experiences to see the old situation in a new light. You complete it. You resolve it. And because you have cleared a place in your emotional body, there is room for this higher awareness to take root. When you have purified the river of emotion that greatly determines the experiences you are capable of, the healing becomes more deeply integrated into every aspect of your being.

Another important reason to clear unresolved emotions from the past is that these feelings create filters that distort your perception. This affects the quality of your relationships and also the possible futures you can create with the people in your life.

Distorted perception, to state the obvious, means you will see things that aren't there and *not* see things that are there. You may think you know what is *really* going on, but you don't. You misread people's intentions and assign character traits to others that are inaccurate.

Feelings create filters that distort your perception.

You can imagine that you are all alone and no one really cares for you when in truth, you are deeply loved and appreciated. You can imagine that others aren't trustworthy when they are. You can feel that you are in danger when you aren't. Distorted perceptions can also lead you to trust people who will take advantage of you or to give your power to other people or organizations because you don't see yourself accurately. Distorted perception is at the root of almost all of your relationship problems.

If you are misperceiving a situation, you can't trust yourself to make wise choices based on a true reality. Making sound choices is one of the most important abilities you have to create your life the way you want it, and one of the most difficult things for humans to do is to see clearly without any distortion. This means getting rid of the distortion factor is a very high priority. Every time you use the CURE you diminish the vault of unconscious material that leads to distorted perception.

One process of misperception is called *projection*, which means unconsciously putting your own ideas or impulses, especially the ones you think are bad, on someone else. In other words, what you don't want to see in yourself, you tend to see and even magnify in others.

Projection is the mechanism of externalizing your internal conflicts. You don't want to see it in yourself because it *feels* bad to see it. The more unresolved feelings you have warehoused in your emotional body, the more you tend to project. Feelings about yourself that you don't want to feel are the driving emotional force in most of your judgments about others.

If you can't be a loving witness to your own anger or rage or sadness or fear, you can't be in the presence of other people's intense emotions without your own emotional waters being churned up a bit. But, if you can learn to feel safe and fully present to the broad spectrum of emotions within your own nature, you radiate an invisible web of safety that helps others to talk about their feelings with you.

If you want to be the kind of person who brings out the best in others, creating a safe way to discuss feelings is a vital skill. The more you understand your own feelings, the easier it is to do this for others.

Arguing about feelings is futile. People feel what they feel whether they have the right to or not. People have all kinds of feelings that are unreasonable. It's counterproductive to judge other people's feelings, and if you can learn to have compassion for their feelings, you will be more insightful and effective at resolving conflict with them.

Adopt a Spiritual Perspective

In his essay, "The Perennial Philosophy," esteemed writer and thinker Aldous Huxley describes four central claims of the perennial philosophy, or the common thread of human spiritual understanding:

♦ The world and all its creatures are expressions of an underlying divine reality.

♦ By appropriate training, humans can come to know this reality.

♦ People can learn to recognize their unity with this divine reality.

♦ Finally, the recognition of the divine reality as the true nature of a human being is the highest goal of human existence.

In our modern culture, people tend to identify with their personality and their various roles. The reality they see with their eyes and experience through the other senses is so compelling it often obscures the invisible spiritual truth of their own divine nature.

However, there are many spiritual disciplines and various personal development workshops and trainings that can help you expand your sense of self to include the ineffable beauty and power of your true, essential self. You can learn to taste your oneness with the ocean of divine joy and wisdom that lives beneath the rolling wave of your own consciousness. This intentional, expansive awareness may be considered spiritual development or conscious evolution.

Barbara Marx Hubbard, a renowned futurist and author of *Conscious Evolution*, states, "Conscious evolution begins when we make the conscious choice to no longer live in separation from the

Source of our own being." This can occur when you regularly attune yourself to your spiritual nature.

It is important for you to have a spiritual practice that gives you access to a divine reality. There is no one-size-fits-all method. You must discover for yourself what practices there are and which ones work best for you. Having a toolkit of practices that tend to the mind, body, and emotions, as well as give you ongoing personal experience of spiritual truth, is necessary when you choose to travel the path of enlightened awareness and spiritual development.

Spiritual Beings Having a Human Experience

As a spiritual being having a human experience, you are biologically and psychologically designed to evolve. An irresistible force compels you to become more, to continually expand your horizons intellectually, emotionally, and spiritually. Practicing the CURE helps you cooperate with and honor this force in your life.

Conflict can be viewed as a way of developing your spiritual muscles so that you grow stronger spiritually. Think weight training. When you want to build your physical muscles, you need something for your muscles to push against, to build strength. The greater the resistance from the weight, usually the more growth you achieve.

The suffering that comes with conflict is like the weight. (Perhaps you have heard the Chinese pictographs for crisis and opportunity are the same, which illustrates their unity.) In challenging times, when you feel you are at the limit of your knowledge and skill, you are catalyzed to grow, become more, expand your abilities. In this process of expansion, you access parts of yourself that were dormant. Just as the stress of the weight for the bodybuilder brings forth a stronger muscle, the stress of conflict can bring forth a greater measure of spiritual maturity and strength.

As these latent capacities emerge, and you recognize deeper spiritual truths, you accelerate your personal and spiritual development. Just as the giant oak tree is hidden inside the tiny acorn, your divine nature is inside you, ready to awaken. Through the dynamic of crisis, you draw forth a higher order of self. From this point of view, upsets, disagreements, and conflict can be seen as spiritual opportunities and evolutionary drivers.

From a spiritual perspective, it can be seen that all events have a purposeful good. Even though calamity may strike, it is often the springboard to greater knowing or wisdom. We have noticed that once the mental and emotional aspects are considered in an upset and relatively cleared up, an authentic spiritual perspective is more readily accessed and integrated.

This perspective is characterized by full personal responsibility and a perception of the *highest spiritual thought*. From this higher vantage point, the perception of victim and victimizer seems to float away like mist in the heat of the sun. Something of value is extracted from this challenge, and the prize is seen as worth everything you have gone through to attain it. You are genuinely grateful for the opportunity, and often, in hindsight, you wouldn't change a thing.

These first couple of chapters have given you the basis of the CURE: our assumptions and a full understanding of radical personal responsibility. The next few chapters will show you how to apply it, step by step. As you begin to practice the CURE, reread some of the earlier chapters from time to time. It will ground you to the most important principles and help make the CURE even more effective as you internalize the new approach to relationships offered here.

CHAPTER THREE

The CURE, Part One: Solo Inquiry

He who looks outside, dreams.
He who looks inside, awakens.

CARL JUNG

The major shift that occurs in practicing the CURE is that when you are resolving conflict between yourself and another, you focus on *your* learning opportunities first. You resist the initial temptation to try and fix the situation that occurred by focusing on the external circumstances or the other person. First handle the internal, then the external. We call this *working from the inside out.*

There are two major keys to handling upsets from the inside out and practicing radical personal responsibility. One key is the fear key. With the fear key, you unlock the secret that reveals what you are really afraid of in that situation, and you neutralize the fear. The other key is the identity key. This key opens your awareness to the impact the upset is having on your sense of self, your identity.

As you practice the CURE, you will see over and over again that fear arises out of the meaning or interpretation you have attached to a situation. Your interpretations flow from your past experiences, or your memories.

Often, when these memories launch into your conscious awareness, you mistake them for true perception or true thinking. But you aren't really seeing things clearly or thinking clearly. You are

45

more like a person in a movie theater when the play button on the projector gets pushed.

It may *feel* as if you are in the jungle swinging in the trees like Tarzan, but you are *really* sitting in a theater watching light projected through film on a giant screen. Your perceptions and feelings seem to contradict what is actually occurring. You can feel as gripped by your memory projections as you can feel carried away in a truly great movie.

As you start to observe your automatic interpretations, you start to notice you have a measure of control over them. You can allow them to follow their own momentum, or you can take a pause to see if this interpretation is fueled by the fear of your conditioned mind, or if it is grounded in the true seeing of your essential self.

Start to observe your automatic interpretations.

If you pause and halt the reactions, you can neutralize your fear and reclaim the power you have given it. You will find that fear doesn't have to run you or your life. You can stop organizing your life to avoid people or situations where your fears can easily be triggered. You will use your fear rather than it using you. You will use your fear to give you clues to where you need to grow.

The basis of all upsets is fear-based emotion. The major force in your emotional pain is a fear-based belief you have about yourself. It is always an idea that is in conflict with your true spiritual nature.

When you feel upset, a negative, fear-based belief you have about yourself has been triggered by the current event. These negative beliefs are usually formed during childhood. You are rarely consciously aware of them as an adult. They live beyond the field of view of your normal attention. Hidden from you, they generate misperceptions, pain, and all of the over-reactions that accompany upsets.

It is difficult for people to observe their automatic interpretive mechanisms, because they work so fast. The CURE slows down the process of mind that goes on below your conscious awareness. When you slow this process down and examine it closely, you discover for yourself that what is hurting you is a negative idea about yourself that has been triggered. This false idea is always in conflict with your true spiritual self.

The source of all your pain comes from misidentifying with a false idea about yourself—in other words, thinking something about yourself that is not true. Don't use this knowledge as a way of talking yourself past your feelings. Don't simply say, "Oh, I've distorted things again. I'm just making it up. No big deal. I'll just ignore it." If you do this, you bypass a learning opportunity vital to your personal growth and healing.

If you are already disquieted, your mind has automatically created a misinterpretation. It is important that you ferret out the source of this distortion. Find the demon, look it in the eye, and call it by name. Then you will find your power over it and remove it from your mental/emotional structure so it won't generate future distortions.

The Light Bulb Moment

After you discover what the specific thought or belief structure is that is causing you to feel upset, you bring it out of the shadows of your mind into the light of awareness, where you challenge its validity. Most of these unknown, negative, limiting ideas you have about yourself will not survive the light of your adult scrutiny.

47

Countless times we have helped people discover the specific thought that was generating the painful interpretation and watched them immediately feel better. In fact, the most common response to naming the exact belief that is causing all the trouble is relief. The next most common response is feeling unusually awake.

People often experience this realization as an enlightenment experience. The light goes on: You can see the truth, and it is unmistakable, shining from your eyes. You become visibly more vibrant. A calmness spreads through your being, and you are bathed in peace. Recognizing the real troublemaker, seeing it isn't the current situation generating this unpleasantness but instead it's this old, seemingly unrelated memory laced with unresolved feelings, brings with it a new sense of freedom and control.

Spontaneously your perception reorganizes itself into a higher order of truth. You don't seem to take the upsetting situation so personally anymore. Your ability to see what is *really* going on empowers you to see new solutions and take new steps.

Albert Einstein has often been quoted as saying, "You can't solve problems on the same level at which they were created." The CURE can help you move to a higher level of perception so new choices and solutions are available. This is power!

Since most upsets are an activation of unresolved pain from the past, there is great value in looking deeper than the obvious. The trick, of course, is figuring out exactly how to do that.

How the CURE Works

Here is an overview of what you will be accomplishing by using the CURE.

1. You will objectify your internal experience so you may look at it more easily. And you will have the opportunity to vent without creating any undesirable consequences in your relationships with other people.

2. You will become aware of the driving emotional forces in your upset and neutralize their power if appropriate.

3. You will find and begin to resolve the root cause of your upset.

4. You will create understanding and compassion for yourself.

5. You will assume responsibility for your part in the upset and become clear on what needs to be changed to help prevent recurrences of this kind of upset.

6. You will see the problem as a specific opportunity to learn, grow, and evolve.

7. You will develop a positive action plan for resolving the immediate upset, as necessary.

8. You will celebrate your accomplishment!

Instructions for Part One, Solo Inquiry

When you are upset, spend time alone as soon as possible to closely examine what is going on with you internally. The following steps are available in worksheet form on page 153, to be used when you're ready to employ the CURE with a specific upset.

Step 1. I am feeling: Write down all the feelings, both emotional and physical, that you are having because of this upset.

Step 2. I am thinking: Write down all the thoughts running through your head concerning this upset.

Step 3. I am upset because: Write a brief description of exactly what you are upset about. It is best to state it simply in one or two sentences.

Step 4. My fear in this upset is: Since fear is the basis of all upsets, get clear on what your biggest fear is in this upset and write it down.

Step 5a. How does this upset impact my private and/or public identity? (How do I think or feel about myself? How might others think or feel about me because of this situation?) Whenever you have upsets, your sense of self is impacted in two ways: the way you think and feel about yourself and the way you imagine others will think or feel about you. Write down the impact this upset may be having on your personal self-image and your reputation with others.

Step 5b. What does it mean about me that . . . ? You begin by completing this question either with your fear in the upset or the brief description of what you are upset about. For example, if you were upset because a friend was not returning your phone calls, you might ask yourself, "What does it mean about me that Laura isn't returning my phone calls?" or if your fear in the upset was Laura is angry with you, you would ask, "What does it mean about me that Laura is angry with me?" Whichever one you begin with, you keep asking the same question, "What does it mean about me that . . . ?" with each response to the question. This path of questioning reveals the trail of automatic lightning-speed interpretations that have resulted in you feeling upset.

We cannot emphasize enough how much the *perceived* impact on your sense of self is distorting your perceptions and driving your emotions. Most of our students consider this step to be the centerpiece of the whole CURE process.

Asking "What does it mean about me?" slows down the automatic, unconscious interpretive mechanism that generates misperceptions, miscommunications, and misunderstandings. The major force in your emotional pain is caused by a thought you have about yourself, not by anything outside of you. The thought about yourself is part of *your* structure. This step in the process reveals the thought from your subconscious mind that is causing you pain.

Asking yourself the same question over and over again reveals this thought. Each response to the question leads you closer to the core thought that is causing you pain. You ask the same question of each response until you get to what feels like the ultimate answer. We call this your *bottom-line thought*.

Your bottom-line thought is the core thought causing you pain. It is a thought out of harmony with your higher self. It is a thought that feels true but is false. It is an untruth that has become a hidden part of your psychological structure.

Sometimes bottom-line thoughts are heavily defended, meaning a part of you wants to protect you from remembering you ever had this thought or the feeling that goes with it. Sometimes it might take someone helping you through the process the first couple of times to build safety and confidence, or you may need to remind yourself that whatever gets revealed in the process is not the ultimate truth about you, but an incomplete understanding of an experience from your past.

Always state your bottom-line thought in an "I" sentence, because it is a thought *you* have about yourself. You will come to recognize your bottom-line thoughts because:

◆ the emotional pain gets more intense when you first think the thought,

◆ or you have a physical reaction like tightness in the chest, neck, shoulders, an upset stomach, etc.,

◆ or you keep repeating the same thought over and over again,

◆ or you simply have an "ah ha!" that feels clear and true to you.

This bottom-line thought has power and force in your life and relationships because it generates an emotional filter through which you tend to hear everything other people say to you, causing you to misinterpret or over-react.

Bottom-line thoughts are typically born in your childhood and come from one or more of the following issues:

◆ **Abandonment**, the fear that you will be left all alone

◆ **Control**, the fear that you will be controlled

◆ **Unlovability**, the fear that you are fundamentally flawed and unlovable

◆ **Exclusion**, the fear of being left out or that you don't belong

◆ **Vulnerability**, the fear that you are not safe

- **Failure**, the fear that you are a fraud and undeserving of success

- **Perfectionism**, the fear that you will never be good enough

- **Entitlement**, the fear that if you aren't given special treatment, your needs will never be satisfied.

Below are some examples of typical bottom-line thoughts and typical mistakes people sometimes make in wording their bottom-line thought.

Examples of bottom-line thoughts:

- *I'm not lovable.*
- *I'm not good enough.*
- *I can't have what I want.*
- *I deserve to be punished.*
- *I cause pain to others.*
- *I'm not important.*
- *I'm bad.*
- *I can't trust people.*
- *I'll always be alone.*
- *I'm a failure.*
- *I'll die.*

Examples of how not to do it:

- *Others don't care about me.*
- *People think I'm bad.*
- *My father doesn't love me.*
- *John will leave me.*
- *People reject me.*
- *People don't understand me.*
- *My mother is controlling.*
- *Men can't be trusted.*
- *Everyone else gets to win, never me.*
- *People want to destroy me.*

Your bottom-line thought is a simple statement. It is not a complex exposition. If your bottom-line thought sounds like something a college professor might say, it is safe to bet you are off the mark.

Look a little deeper and key in to the emotional component. Usually the bottom line is expressed with a childlike directness. Remember, it is a thought about you, not about anyone else.

Step 6. My bottom-line thought is: Write down your bottom-line thought.

IMPORTANT: Your bottom-line thought is only a thought you have about yourself; it is not The Truth of who you are.

It is a good idea to question the validity of your bottom-line thought. This thought is not to be believed but challenged and changed! As you change your thinking, you change your interpretations and your experience and the way you react to others in the future.

WARNING!

YOU MAY EXPERIENCE SIGNIFICANT RELIEF AT THIS POINT,
BUT DO NOT STOP UNTIL YOU HAVE FINISHED THE ENTIRE EXERCISE!
THERE IS STILL SOME IMPORTANT WORK TO DO.

Step 7. What resources can I use to heal and resolve my bottom-line thought? Insight is not enough to resolve something. It is only the first step and is almost completely useless without proper action. You should have a toolkit of resources you can use to help you in these situations. You select from your healing resources and write down all the possible ways you can think of to heal, resolve, upgrade, or transform your bottom-line thought.

Examples might be affirmations, new choices, belief-change work, visualization, or other healing modalities like Relationship Energy Repatterning tools (there is more information on this in the next chapter). Choose the ones on which you will take action.

If you do not already have a toolkit of reliable and trusted resources, then we strongly recommend you get a coach or counselor to help you. You do not have to do this all alone. Among the resources in your toolkit can be coaches and other expert help from those who have special skill in facilitating internal change.

Step 8. The earliest I can remember feeling this way is: Look into your past to discover where your bottom-line thought comes from. You will probably get a thought or an image from your past. Trust it and write it down. It may not be the absolute earliest, but it is taking you in the right direction and is training your thinking. This brings you insight, understanding, and compassion.

Step 9. The thoughts, feelings, and attitudes I hold that contribute to this current upset are: Now, look for any thoughts, feelings, or attitudes you hold that may have contributed to the upset and write them down. This is to help you take responsibility for the part *your* consciousness played in an upset occurring. This awareness helps you defuse the negative factors that can create future upsets. Explore thoughts, feelings, and attitudes about power, men and women, trust, safety, getting what you want, feeling valued, what is right and what is wrong, fairness, etc.

Step 10. The learning/growth opportunities for me in this upset are: Speculate about what you could be learning in this situation. Perhaps it is to resolve something from your past or to learn something new that will take you to the future you want. Try looking at this from the perspective of your higher self. How might your higher self be using this situation to help you grow in wisdom, compassion, and spiritual awareness?

Step 11. What requests can I make to be responsible for my own needs? How can I turn my complaints into requests and generate cooperation? Within every complaint is a request. Clarify what your requests could be and write them down. In healthy adult relationships, we are each responsible for our own needs. And part of that responsibility is making clear requests that inspire others to cooperate with us in getting our needs satisfied.

(You can tell the difference between a demand and a request when the other person says no. If it was a request, you can accept it. If it was a demand, you make the other person wrong for saying no.)

Step 12. Steps I can take to resolve this current upset are:
Write down the specific action steps you can take to work it out with
the other person or people involved. These are usually more than
simply making requests. Perhaps it is to institute a new policy at
work, communicate your side of the story, apologize, acknowledge
your responsibility in the situation, ask for forgiveness or offer it, etc.

Step 13. How can I or we celebrate this learning experience? It
is important for you to reward yourself for choosing a new way of
thinking and behaving when you've been upset. This is a vital step in
retraining your mind and body and is often minimized or completely
overlooked. You usually continue with behavior that gets rewarded. It
is more effective if the reward is immediate and visible to your body's
eyes. Subtle, long-term rewards don't work! What can you do to
celebrate your accomplishment? Write it down and schedule it. Then
follow through and do it!

How can you celebrate?

That's it! You're done with Part One. If you are having an upset
with someone who knows about this tool and knows how to use it,
then you move on to Part Two, the dialogue.

Often, though, after you do your inner work you see there isn't
much left to do, if anything, with another person. The upset was
completely internal. You tuck the value from this learning experience
under your arm and trot lightly down the path of your life.

Or perhaps the upset didn't involve another person at all. Maybe
you were upset with your car or your bills. Using the CURE has still
revealed parts of your internal structure that leave you vulnerable to
outside stimuli.

If you have used the CURE for an upset involving someone who doesn't know about this method, you are still much more prepared to have a solution-based conversation that is free from unwanted emotional undercurrents. You will have gained a deeper understanding of yourself and already transformed adversity into a benefit.

There are many layers of truth revealed in the CURE process. Many of the answers to your questions will depend on your level of self-awareness. We recommend that you save your CURE worksheets. You may be able to see more deeply into the issues after a little time has passed, and they serve as a valuable documentation of your personal growth.

The worksheets serve as training wheels for your mind. After a while, you will outgrow the need for them. Whenever an upset gets triggered for you, you will automatically start asking yourself these important questions. You will neutralize the core emotional drivers and stop upsets from escalating. You will see all upsets as gifts, which you skillfully unwrap, only to find yourself richer because of them.

Two Sample Upsets and CURE Worksheets

You should look at life unmasked,
in the mirror of your experiences . . . Look at
the perpetual current of emotions and
thoughts that arise in you . . .
Seek understanding with your highest
intelligence, wisdom, love,
and vision.

PARAMAHANSA YOGANANDA

In this first upset, Joe averts a conflict by using the CURE with someone who isn't familiar with this process at all. His CURE worksheet follows his story.

"

As I was coming into my office last week, I passed Kathy in the hall. I like Kathy. She's smart and enthusiastic.

"Hi, Kathy. Great to see you! How are things?"

"Fine," she clipped, with a glare that could melt your bones. She moved on down the hall like a locomotive. I stood there, speechless and stunned.

I couldn't imagine what was going on with her. I'd thought we were developing a friendship. But from out of nowhere she's got an "attitude." I talked to one of our co-workers later that day.

"Nathan, have you noticed anything 'off' with Kathy lately?"

"Only when you're around. As soon as you enter a room, she gets very quiet. Something is definitely going on. Why don't you ask her?"

"Yeah, I guess I better," I said, feeling the knot in my stomach.

"I hate confrontations," I grumbled to myself. I wanted to talk to her about it but it seemed pretty risky, especially after the hall incident. I was hoping that whatever it was would just blow over in a few days, but if anything, it got worse. I knew I was going to have to do something because the emotional tension was distracting the rest of the team. But every time I thought to initiate a dialogue, I'd get nervous and get this tight feeling in my gut. So I'd decide not to follow through.

I was getting angry and impatient, and then after another week I remembered the CURE and decided to give it a go. The real turning point in the exercise happened when I saw where my bottom line came from. It had been a long time since my dad died. I was only five years old. But, when I asked question 8, "When is the earliest you can remember feeling this way?" the memory exploded into my awareness.

My mom had come completely undone after my dad died. Her doctors told her she was having a nervous breakdown and she needed some time to rest and heal. She felt the best thing she could do for me was to put me somewhere where she knew I would be loved and taken care of. So she sent me to live with my grandparents.

She tells me it was for only four months—but it felt like forever. For me, it was like having both my parents die. I remember feeling so hurt and out of control. It was as if she didn't care about me. If I had been important to her, she would have wanted me to be with her, right?

Just after the memory started coming, I could see how similar so many of the feelings were to what had happened when I wanted to talk to Kathy. It just seemed that if I were important enough to Kathy she would have initiated a dialogue, rather than ignoring me. I felt like giving up before I even tried to talk to her. I "knew" she didn't care about my thoughts or feelings anyway.

Then it was like a split-screen effect; the story about my mom and dad was running on one side, and the movie about Kathy was playing on the other. After I was just there watching all this in my mind for a while, it occurred to me I was jumping to a lot of conclusions with Kathy. There were several other reasons she could be acting the way she was, but I hadn't been able to even think along this line because I had gotten so triggered by her behavior.

After I did some "change work" on some of the decisions I had made when my mom sent me to live with my grandparents, I felt calm and clear-minded. I was also feeling optimistic. I knew I was going to be able to talk about whatever was going on and we could work it out. All the anxiety about it was gone.

The next morning I walked over to Kathy's office and poked my head in.

"Are you busy?"

"Kind of," she replied.

"This will just take a minute. May I?" I asked, assuming permission as I stepped across the threshold. "I don't know what happened in our relationship, but I am feeling awful about it. Can we have a sit-down and see if we can smooth things out?"

Kathy looked at me as she weighed her answer. "I suppose," she said carefully.

"Do you want to do it now or later?" I asked, trying to keep my voice warm.

She paused again. "Well, I guess now is as good a time as any. Have a seat."

I sat down in the chair across from her desk. "Well, first I should say I don't know if I did something to offend you, but whatever happened, I want us to work this out so we both feel good about it. Is that okay by you?"

Kathy visibly relaxed.

"I think I need to know from you what is going on, because I am clueless. It seems to me we were doing just great, and then all of a sudden, things got, well, strained. I've spent the last week not knowing how to approach you to find out what happened."

"You're kidding, right?" she said with just a touch of sarcasm.

"No, really, Kathy. I don't know what is going on."

"Well, I didn't much appreciate that remark you made at the Progress Presentation."

"Remark?"

"And I quote, 'Now that Kathy has laid the groundwork, let's think of who is the BEST presenter for the launch.'" She paused. The word best was still ringing in the air.

I sat there taking it in. And the light dawned. "Did you think I was saying you weren't good enough to be the presenter?"

"It sure sounded like it to me," she said, keeping her emotion under control.

"I didn't mean that, Kathy. I guess I can see how you may have heard it that way, but that's not what I was saying—at all," I added with emphasis.

"I was just saying, this phase is complete, let's get prepared for the next phase. I hadn't ruled you out as a presenter. But I don't think we should assume that whoever does the research should automatically lead out on the presentation. I think we need to take it on a case-by-case basis. That's all I meant."

"So, you would consider me as the presenter?"

"Of course!"

"Okay. That feels better. I thought the way you said it you had dismissed me altogether."

"No, not at all." I sat there smiling at her while everything fell together in my mind. "I think we have had a major misunderstanding. What do you think?"

"I guess we have. You must have thought I have been acting pretty weird."

"I was completely mystified."

"I'm really sorry, Joe. I thought you were turning out to be one of those 'boys club' kind of guys." She hesitated before adding, "I'm the only female on the team. I guess I jumped to the wrong conclusion."

"Hmmm. I think so. We don't know each other very well yet. So let me say, just for the record, I don't have any gender bias going on. I apologize if the way I spoke upset you. I didn't mean anything by it. I also think there is something we can each learn from the situation. For me, I've learned not to wait so long to clear things up. Misunderstandings happen between people even with the best of intentions. And I never could have figured out what was truly going on because I didn't have all the information. You had some of it. I should have initiated this conversation rather than waiting for you to do it."

I paused to let this sink in. She didn't seem to be taking the cue for her own responsibility, so I just asked, "What do you think you can learn?" I took special care to keep my voice warm and curious.

She reflected a moment before she spoke. "The same thing. It never occurred to me that I had misread you. So I saw no reason to check out my perception. And I see that I should have."

"Is there any reason that you would have jumped to the conclusion you did?"

Kathy chose her words very carefully. "I've been competing in a man's world all my life. I think it has made me, mmmm, a bit defensive. I misjudged you, Joe. I'm sorry."

"Apology accepted," I smiled. "So let's make a deal. If anything ever happens again, we'll check in with each other to make sure we've both got all the facts. Right?"

"You bet. Thanks for this." Her eyes twinkled in that way I remembered so well. Kathy stood up and came around her desk to offer her hand. We gave each other a warm handshake. It was a good connection.

All in all, it was a valuable learning experience. Now that it's over, I can almost say I'm glad it happened. Kathy and I are getting along well now. We are more relaxed with each other than before the upset.

A couple of times I have wondered if it would have turned out as well if I hadn't done the CURE, and I don't think it would have. Because I was able to see what my part of the equation was, I was able to take some different actions than I would have otherwise. Seeing the piece about my dad's death and being sent to live with my grandparents helped me understand why I was feeling the way I was. Looking at the decisions I had made when I was a kid let me see I had some work to do on myself. After I did that, it helped me be more relaxed and curious about what was really going on. Before that I was just trying to protect myself.

I got to learn some valuable information about Kathy, too. I think it is important to know the filters that other people see through. Especially when you work with them. You can't expect they will always be able to see them for themselves. But, if you can see them, it can stop you from taking it all so personally.

"

The CURE™ Worksheet
The Conscious Upset Resolution Exercise

Part One, Solo Inquiry (To Do Alone)

Name: *Joe*   **Date:** *March 12, 2002*

OBJECTIFY YOUR INTERNAL EXPERIENCE AND VENT

1. I am feeling:
irritated, hurt, confused, like I want to break things, my head hurts, stomach tight

2. I am thinking:
Kathy is so arrogant. This is ridiculous! This should not be happening. Who the hell does she think she is! I don't have to take this. This whole thing is stupid. I hate this. How can we work this out? There has to be a way.

BECOME AWARE OF YOUR DRIVING EMOTIONAL FORCES

3. I am upset because:
Kathy won't work through this problem with me. She barely even speaks to me.

4. My fear in this upset is:
I won't be able to work well with her anymore.

65

5a. How does this upset impact my private and/or public identity? (How do I think or feel about myself? How might others think or feel about me because of this situation?)
People won't think I am a good team player (maybe??). People will think this upset is my fault and that I am wrong.

5b. What does it mean about me that . . . ? (Use the reply to question 3 or 4, or both.)
...Kathy won't work through this problem with me?
It means I am not important.

NOTE: All the following questions are stated with *if*, because they are only interpretations, not facts.

What does it mean about me if I 'm not important?
I won't be respected.

What does it mean about me if I won't be respected?
I will feel bad.

What does it mean about me if I will feel bad?
I won't be happy.

What does it mean about me if I won't be happy?
I won't get what I want.

What does it mean about me if I won't get what
I want?
I'll be a failure.

What does it mean about me if I'll be a failure?
I won't get what I want.

Joe recognizes his bottom-line thought is *I won't get what I want.* He can tell because every time he thinks it, his eyes tear up. He decides to stop here and track his responses to question 4 to see if something different comes up.

What does it mean about me that I am afraid
I won't be able to work with Kathy anymore? It
means I'll be miserable.

What does it mean about me if I'll be miserable?
I won't be productive.

What does it mean about me if I won't be
productive?
I won't be respected.

What does it mean about me if I won't be
respected?
I won't get what I want.

At this point, Joe stops. There is that same thought again—*I won't get what I want*—with the same teary response. He looks back over all the responses to the question, "What does it mean about me . . . ?" It is clear to him the thought activating his pain is *I won't get what I want because I'm not respected.* He writes it down under number 6.

Because he won't be writing the question, "What does it mean about me . . . ?" over and over again on his worksheet, and he will be writing only his responses, his worksheet will look like this:

5b. What does it mean about me that . . . ?
(Reply to question 3:) Kathy won't work through this problem with me?
    I'm not important.
    I won't be respected.
    I will feel bad.
    I won't be happy.
    I won't get what I want.
    I'll be a failure.
    I won't get what I want.

(Reply to question 4:) I'm afraid I won't be able to work with Kathy anymore.
    I'll be miserable.
    I won't be productive.
    I won't be respected.
    I won't get what I want.

6. My bottom-line thought is:
I won't get what I want because I'm not respected.

Warning!
Do not stop here just because you feel relief!

TAKE STEPS TO RESOLVE THE CAUSE OF THE UPSET

7. What resources can I use to heal and resolve my bottom-line thought? (Affirmations, new choice statements, belief-change work, energy psychology techniques, and other healing/transformational modalities)

Affirmations: I am highly respected and I feel it. I am supported in having what I want. People want me to have what I want.

Choice Statement: Even when others won't communicate with me, I can choose to know that I have the power to create what I want and respect myself.

Write a "vent letter" to defuse and release my intense feelings and then burn it.

Make a list of five times when I have felt respected by other people and have gotten what I wanted.

Use the tapping technique from Relationship Energy Repatterning to diminish my upset feelings.

CREATE UNDERSTANDING AND COMPASSION

8. The earliest I can remember feeling this way is:
When I was five years old and my dad died. My mom sent me to live with my grandparents. I didn't see or talk to my mom for a long time. It

seemed like if my needs were respected that wouldn't have happened.

BE RESPONSIBLE FOR YOUR PART AND CHANGE WHAT DOESN'T WORK

9. The thoughts, feelings, and attitudes I hold that contribute to this current upset are:

I get anxious when people freeze me out. I shut down when people get upset with me and I wait for them to come to me. I think people should see things my way and I get short-tempered when they don't.

SEE THE PROBLEM AS A LEARNING/HEALING OPPORTUNITY

10. The learning/growth opportunities for me in this upset are:

To further heal the pain around my dad's death and being sent away. To stop waiting for people to come to me. If something is going on, I can take the initiative to clear it up.

CREATE A POSITIVE ACTION PLAN

11. What requests can I make to be responsible for my own needs? How can I turn my complaint into a request and generate cooperation?

Ask people (specifically Kathy, Mark, Jason, and Patricia) to talk as soon as possible after a disagreement, so they know how I prefer to handle things.

12. Steps I can take to resolve this current upset are:

I can send Kathy a memo requesting that we meet soon to work this out. Let her know I see how I can handle things differently in the future.

REWARD AND REINFORCE
THE LEARNING AND HEALING PROCESS

13. How can I/we celebrate this learning experience?
I will invite Kathy for a long lunch or a latté. Later I will take a Jacuzzi and listen to my favorite music. And I can acknowledge myself for completing this worksheet.

Next, Bonnie, who provides our second example, hates being single. She uses the CURE to understand the pattern she's created in her life and to generate solutions she knows will work for her. Her CURE worksheet follows her story.

"
_____

I am so mad at myself I could scream. What an idiot I am! Why did I sit there like such a "nice girl" when the son-of-a-bitch lied to me? If he had told me what he really looked like, I never would have gone out with him. He's at least twenty years older than I am, balding and fat. I just wish I could die.

I remember the day I came home from my first date with someone I had met at an online dating service. I was in tears. I wanted to crawl under the covers and never come out again. I just sat there rocking myself back and forth, crying and crying, a giant hill of used Kleenex piling up beside me. It would have been pretty funny if it hadn't felt so tragic. It was so cliché, the classic date from hell.

I'm thirty-three years old, and I've never been married. All my sisters are married, even my younger one. They are always trying to fix me up. It's embarrassing. I feel like a "desperate case."

I don't think I should be embarrassed to still be single, but the cold hard truth is I am. I'm mortified. It feels like everyone I meet must feel sorry for me. They must know there's something very wrong with me or I wouldn't still be single.

Putting on that brave smile and telling everyone how "I love my life" is wearing pretty damned thin. Most of the time I'm miserable. Actually, that's not true. Most of the time, I'm fine. Every once in a while I'm desperately miserable. And when that happens my whole life feels pathetic.

I've had this deep lonely feeling most of my life. From using the CURE a dozen or more times, I know it comes from my relationship with my dad. He left when I was real young, and I still haven't healed from it yet. Being single and looking for a mate seems to be the perfect set-up to "work it out." But I'm getting pretty damned tired of seeing it over and over again.

So now I know when I'm yearning for the man of my dreams to come carry me off to happily ever after, I'm mostly feeling the younger part of me that misses my daddy and wants him to come home and swing me 'round and 'round and call me his "special baby girl," knowing somehow he can make all the pain go away.

Okay, I can see it. When that old feeling comes I know what it really is. Big deal! Oops, there goes the self-pity thing again. I'm just disappointed that the awareness hasn't made the pain go away completely. Sure, it's getting better. It isn't as debilitating as it was, nor does it happen as often as it used to, but it's still there. Patience is hard for me. I don't want to be patient. I want what I want, when I want it, which is NOW!!

God, I sound like such a child! Well, I feel like a child. But I have to grow up. Being a grown-up is about facing facts and dealing with them. Here are the facts. I'm a thirty-three-year old woman who still hasn't resolved her feelings of abandonment when her dad left. I hate being single and I am single. If I want to create a good marriage in my future, I'm going to have to be patient and make a series of wise choices. Feeling desperately lonely won't help me do that. This problem isn't going to go away any time soon. So, I have to find a way to be smart and keep taking steps toward what I really want. Not get discouraged, but focus on the good things in my life and try to learn patience. If I can't learn to do this, I'm sunk.

I'm just going to have to learn how to use this difficult stage in my life as a "growth opportunity," even if it's hard to do. It's great to have a tool like the CURE. It's not a magic pill, but it's the next best thing. It helps a lot when the going gets tough, and when I'm in my right mind I can see the light at the end of the tunnel.

Someday, I will have healed my broken heart about my dad leaving. I will have learned to love and accept myself whether I am single or in a relationship. I will have learned I don't need a man to love myself or to be happy. I will have learned that I truly am lovable and I deserve to be happy. I will be grown up enough to put as much attention on giving love as trying to get it. I will have learned that I have a lot to offer a man and that when I finally connect with my true love, I'll know he is as lucky to love me as I am to love him.

And, until that day, I'm going to use the CURE every time I feel discouraged or impatient or upset. That's as grown up as I can be right now! And how grown up is that?

”

The CURE™ Worksheet
The Conscious Upset Resolution Exercise

Part One, Solo Inquiry (To Do Alone)

Name: *Bonnie*   **Date:** *October 5, 2001*

OBJECTIFY YOUR INTERNAL EXPERIENCE AND VENT

1. I am feeling:
frustrated, tricked, angry, despairing, sweaty, puffy. I've been crying. My head hurts.

2. I am thinking:
Why did I go out with that guy? What a loser! I hate dating! I hate being single. Why me? I can't do this anymore. I want to crawl in a hole. I want the pain to stop. Somebody please help me!!!!

BECOME AWARE OF YOUR
DRIVING EMOTIONAL FORCES

3. I am upset because:
My date with this guy sucked!!!!

4. My fear in this upset is:
I will never find my true love.

5a. How does this upset impact my private and/or public identity? (How do I think or feel about myself? How might others think or feel about me because of this situation?)
People will think I'm a loser. My girlfriends will feel sorry for me.

5b. What does it mean about me that . . . ? (Use the reply to question 3 or 4, or both.)
. . . I will never find my true love.
I'll always be lonely.

NOTE: All the following questions are stated with *if*, because they are only interpretations, not facts.

What does it mean about me <u>if</u> I'll always be lonely?
I'll be unhappy.
No one will want me because I'll be so pathetic.
I'll be all alone.
I'll never get what I really want.
I'm a loser.
No one will want me.
I'll always be alone and lonely.

6. My bottom-line thought is:
I'll always be alone and lonely.

WARNING!
DO NOT STOP HERE JUST BECAUSE YOU FEEL RELIEF!

TAKE STEPS TO RESOLVE THE CAUSE OF THE UPSET

7. What resources can I use to heal and resolve my bottom-line thought? (Affirmations, new choice statements, belief-change work, energy psychology techniques, and other healing/transformational modalities.)
Affirmations: I am destined to live happily ever after with the man of my dreams. (This

certainty helps me to be patient and enjoy the process of finding him.)

Choice statement: Even though I feel all alone, I choose to know I am connected to an infinite source of divine love that can heal my broken heart.

Write a "vent letter" to defuse and release my intense feelings and then burn it.

Use the RER (Relationship Energy Repatterning) tapping techniques to clear the emotional pain pumping through my system.

Work on my Relationship Creation project to lift my spirits.

CREATE UNDERSTANDING AND COMPASSION

8. The earliest I can remember feeling this way is:
After my parents got a divorce and mom had to go to work. I was alone a lot then. I missed my dad terribly. There was no one to comfort me.

BE RESPONSIBLE FOR YOUR PART AND CHANGE WHAT DOESN'T WORK

9. The thoughts, feelings, and attitudes I hold that contribute to this current upset are:
Men don't want me. Maybe there is something wrong with me. I don't want to wait anymore. My impatience is making me desperate, so I am not as selective in dating the way I should be.

I'm afraid I'll never have the love I want, and it is easy for me to feel sorry for myself.

SEE THE PROBLEM AS A LEARNING/HEALING OPPORTUNITY

10. The learning/growth opportunities for me in this upset are:
To heal my desperation for romantic love. To develop self-confidence and the kind of strength of character that comes from being persistent. To heal my grief around my parents' split. To deepen my spiritual connection so that my peace and well-being can be an attractive force for the kind of man I really want.

CREATE A POSITIVE ACTION PLAN

11. What requests can I make to be responsible for my own needs? How can I turn my complaint into a request and generate cooperation?
Ask more questions before I accept a date - to make sure they are who they make themselves out to be. Make a change on my online profile clarifying how important honesty and integrity are to me, so I screen out the creepy ones. Ask myself what I am really looking for in a mate and figure out how to pose that as a question when I am screening prospective dates. Ask myself what I really <u>don't want</u> and communicate this to prospective dates so they can disqualify themselves.

12. Steps I can take to resolve this current upset are:
Forgive this guy for not respecting himself enough to represent himself accurately. Write a

letter from my higher self to that part of me that is hurting and afraid, to reassure her that things are in the process of turning out and she just needs to be patient. Also, use this time as a single person to heal more deeply; that way I will be ready when my true love and I finally meet one another.

REWARD AND REINFORCE
THE LEARNING AND HEALING PROCESS

13. How can I/we celebrate this learning experience?
Have breakfast on the veranda tomorrow while listening to my Italian Arias CD.

Mining the Spiritual Gold:
Clearing Your Issue

The grapes of my body can only become wine
After the winemaker tramples me.
I surrender my spirit like grapes to the trampling
So my innermost heart can blaze and dance with joy.
Although the grapes go on weeping blood and sobbing,
"I cannot bear any more anguish, any more cruelty,"
The trampler stuffs cotton in his ears:
"I am not working in ignorance.
You can deny me if you want, you have every excuse,
but it is I who am the Master of this Work.
And when, through my Passion, you reach Perfection,
You will never be done praising my name."

RUMI

One of our teachers likes to use stories to help us learn. He is known as The Storyteller. We'd like to share one of his tales with you.

Once there was a child wandering along the seashore, collecting all the wonderful things he found there. There were shells and polished rocks and all manner of interesting and marvelous things. With each new treasure he would absorb its wonder, then put it in a bucket he carried with him.

After a while, he came upon a different shoreline. It sparkled as far as his eyes could see. He felt a new sense of joy as he watched the dancing particles of light shimmer beautifully and mysteriously. His enthusiasm pulled him forward. He could hardly wait to explore this new place.

Soon he came upon a dazzling sapphire, and then he saw rubies and diamonds scattered across the sand. He was beside himself with delight. He started collecting all the most exquisite gems until his hands could hold no more. He went to put them in his bucket, but there was no more room.

He was going to have to make more room in the bucket for his new treasures. So he started to sort through the contents of his bucket, and the things he didn't want anymore he threw back into the sea. He gave a great sigh of satisfaction as he gazed at the landscape ahead of him. New and wondrous treasures awaited him, and he started off with an empty bucket in which to collect them.

In this story, you could see yourself as the child and the bucket as your consciousness. The shoreline represents your life journey, and the treasures are your experiences and beliefs. From time to time, you have to let go of some of the beliefs you have collected to move on.

When you have used the CURE to discover your bottom-line thoughts, you have a healing path before you. Once you've brought what has been holding you back or causing you pain into your conscious awareness, you can begin to experience things newly and see them as they truly are.

The upsets that happen in your life can be seen as your soul's way of showing you which beliefs you need to give up. The CURE helps you get right to the bottom line: those beliefs that restrain you from realizing your highest potential, the ultimate recognition that the divine reality is your own true nature.

When you start to "get" the messages your soul is sending, you are making spiritual progress. If you don't listen to these messages, which often arrive via upsets, they seem to amplify. First the message comes in a small way, but if you don't notice it or you ignore it, the volume has to be turned up, so to speak. That means the upsets get bigger, and if you continue to miss the message, they just keep getting bigger and bigger until your soul gets you to pay attention. If the message shows up as a pebble in the beginning and you step over it without noticing, the next time it shows up as a rock, then a boulder, then a hill, then a mountain. It will continue to get bigger until the only thing you can do is pay attention to it.

Following Through on the CURE

One of the payoffs of spiritual development is you start to read quickly the signals your higher self is sending. Somehow it just makes sense to get the message before you have to be hit over the head by the metaphorical two-by-four! Using the CURE helps you get the message sooner rather than later.

When you discover your bottom-line thought with the CURE, you have to work with it to make a change. Insight is not enough, though it's a great place to start. It's also a good idea to begin your own change work before you go on to Part Two of the CURE. The more personal clarity you can bring to any dialogue, the better.

First you need to see your bottom-line thought for what it is, which can be pretty tricky, really, since it is invisible. Your bottom-line thought is the negative core belief inside a cluster of ideas or thoughts. This cluster is held together by what we call *emotional glue*.

This whole cluster is usually shielded from your awareness by the human phenomenon of denial. It's there to be seen, but you don't want to see it, so you don't. The denial is there to protect you from feeling things you don't want to feel. You can see an illustration of this on page 18.

Imagine if you decided when you were younger, through a series of experiences, that you were never going to be good enough. That (probably unconscious) decision would not have a neutral feeling. That decision would come with all kinds of disturbances, an assortment of pain, sadness, shame, longing, fear, anger, and hurt. A decision like this wouldn't be a simple mental process; it would be fraught with emotion.

When you start to dismantle negative core beliefs, you must deal with the emotional glue that is holding the whole thing together. This means paying attention to feelings you would prefer to ignore. Most people approach emotional healing with a great deal of fear and trepidation. But before you get worried, we have some very good news.

Everything Is Energy

At the most fundamental level, everything is energy, including beliefs, attitudes, and feelings. You can work at changing your beliefs and emotions at the level of energy. There are new tools for "emptying your bucket," if you will, following the metaphor at the beginning of this chapter. These new energy tools are direct and gentle and effective. Once you find a troublemaker belief, you can look to find a more empowering one, such as *my best is good enough* or *I deserve to love and accept myself even if I make mistakes*.

You can intentionally embrace this new positive idea while using energy tools to remove the old mental-emotional structure from your energy field, the energy field that is your mind. This makes emotional healing a whole lot easier than it used to be.

If this sounds too hocus-pocus for you, let us remind you of something. Before Louis Pasteur and his famous Germ Theory, it was unknown that microorganisms, invisible to the naked eye, were the cause of many diseases. His discoveries forever changed the way most diseases are treated.

In his address before the French Academy of Sciences on April 29, 1878 he said, "All things are hidden and obscure if the cause of the phenomena is unknown, but everything is clear if the cause is known." When you understand that mental-emotional distress is primarily caused by invisible perturbations in the energy body, it only makes sense to treat them at that level.

Energy Psychology and Energy Interventions

We refer to the energy body as the *human vibrational matrix*. The expanding knowledge of the human vibrational matrix has given rise to a new field called *energy psychology*, which is an umbrella term used to describe a variety of techniques for resolving a wide range of problems. The term represents the green, growing edge of psychology and the study of emotional health and well-being.

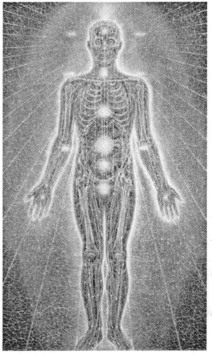

Artwork by Alex Gray. Used with permission.

Energy psychology draws upon the latest breakthroughs in physics and neuroscience, as well as the wisdom of the ages. It provides elegantly simple, non-intrusive yet potent methodologies for communicating with and modifying the body/mind system for desired results. We call these methodologies *energy interventions*.

Energy interventions are regularly used to treat irrational fears (phobias), normal fears and anxieties, unresolved emotions from the past, PTSD (post-traumatic stress disorder), addictions, and relationship pain. We have been using and teaching energy interventions since 1989. You can use them to address any of the issues you uncover as you work with the CURE.

If you want assistance with using any of the tools covered in this chapter, please visit www.EnlightenedPartners.com/energy.html. You'll find information on and help with Relationship Energy Repatterning and more.

Energy psychology focuses on three major interacting systems:

1. pathways (meridians and related acupoints),

2. centers (chakras), and

3. the biofield (aura).

While there are many approaches to working with each of these three aspects independently, energy psychology embraces all three interactive energy systems and teaches treatment approaches for each aspect, facilitating the best possible outcome for you. All three of these interacting systems may be thought of as the human vibrational matrix.

Relationship Energy Repatterning

Relationship Energy Repatterning (RER) does exactly what the name implies: it reconfigures your unconscious patterns of energy that manifest in a variety of unhealthy ways into healthier patterns of attitude, choice, and behavior. RER is used to heal and re-create your mental-emotional structure so that you are able to respond to the challenges in your life the way you would prefer. RER interventions can be used to effectively transform negative patterns with individuals, couples, and groups.

We developed RER specifically for relationship concerns, whether in business, romance, friendships, or family. RER intervenes on all three levels of the human vibrational matrix: the meridian system, the chakra system, and the biofield. RER consists of five different energy interventions.

RER intervenes on all three levels of the human vibrational matrix.

We have synthesized a number of modalities and techniques to create the variety of energy interventions of Relationship Energy Repatterning. They are applied kinesiology, educational kinesiology, Neuro-Linguistic Programming (NLP), Ericksonian hypnosis, breathwork, Emotional Freedom Techniques (EFT), and other meridian-based therapies and energy psychology techniques. RER continues to evolve as we learn more about how personal energy fields affect thinking, choices, and behavior.

You can learn to use some of the interventions for yourself. Some of them are too complex for the average learner, so it is best that you go to a Certified Relationship Energy Repatterning Practitioner. We teach people these techniques in workshops, over the phone in live teleclasses, as well as through recorded online classes where you get the notes and audio recordings via your computer.

We use RER with almost all of our clients, even working over the phone. We teach whole families how to support one another with these simple and powerful techniques. We have been training professional coaches, counselors, and therapists in RER for more than ten years. We offer everything from five-hour teleclasses to week-long certification trainings.

Emotional Freedom Techniques (EFT) encompass some of the primary energy interventions included in the repertoire of techniques making up RER. EFT uses a simple tapping technique on the endpoints of your meridians. Meridians are to your energy body what veins and arteries are to your physical body. Some people think of EFT as acupressure for your emotions. It is very powerful and effective for ninety percent of the people with whom we use it.

With the use of EFT, we are able to work with people effectively over the telephone. EFT is one of the easiest-to-learn energy interventions we use. We can teach you how to use it on yourself so that if you get triggered, you can immediately treat yourself. We consider it the ultimate in self-care, and you can also learn to use it to help other people.

Online, you may listen for free to a recorded class, "Fear Blaster! An Introduction to Emotional Freedom Techniques." Just go to www.EnlightenedPartners.com/energy.html, where you can hear the teleclass in which one of the techniques is demonstrated for people who are learning about it for the first time.

If you decide you want to learn to use one of the techniques right away, click the link for the Emotional Freedom Training, and within minutes you can begin to learn this powerful energy intervention, right through your computer.

❝ ....

My husband doesn't like to talk when he gets upset. He just goes far, far away, deep inside himself, where nobody can get to him. Using the CURE has changed this almost completely.

In the beginning, after we took the CURE class, we would forget to use it. Several days of feeling bad would go by before one of us remembered it. Then we would pull out our worksheets and do Part Two, where you talk about it.

The steps in the worksheet have really helped Michael sort through his thoughts and feelings and then talk to me about them. Before, he didn't know how to do that, so he wouldn't even try. I always felt lonely and shut out whenever he got upset, like there was a big wall between us. Now, we use the CURE almost right away, and it always makes things easier.

Michael came home a month ago with some really bad news. He had been laid off. I could tell he was starting to go into that far away place. We didn't use the CURE at first. We went straight to the RER tapping tool. It worked right away.

Being able to help Michael with tapping was powerful for both of us. For him: because he was able to stay close to me even though he was worried. For me: I was just grateful there was something I could do instead of feeling helpless while I waited for him to come out of his shell.

It was up and down for a couple of weeks and we both used the CURE when the going got tough. When I look back on that time, I know for sure that the whole process of Michael getting laid off and finding a new job was a lot easier because we were able to talk and strategize and work together, rather than letting the pain and fear drive us apart. I have a whole new respect and trust for my husband and the way we handle problems now.

"

Trigger Work

Your bottom-line thought is what gets triggered in an upset. Once you have discovered the bottom-line thought that is generating your unwanted reactions and patterns, it is important to follow through and change it at the energetic level. We call this *trigger work*. Some people think of this as disappearing their "buttons."

We use RER to change your bottom-line thoughts so they no longer produce unpleasant reactions and upsets for you. RER heals and evolves your mental-emotional structure so you don't react negatively to outside stimuli. Same stimuli, different structure, different result.

Your negative mental-emotional structures can be triggered by anything: a look, voice tone, word, gesture, etc. Once your patterns are set in motion, they seem to have a life of their own, issuing forth their predictable commands and tragic effects. But if you can disappear the cause of your triggers, you eradicate the pattern.

Same stimuli, different structure, different result.

Relationships of all kinds are subject to your negative triggers. These triggers ignite automatic perceptions and behaviors. These perceptions are rooted in thoughts of fear, suspicion, and distrust, fierce beliefs about what is "right" and "wrong" according to gender or role, and feelings of emotional survival, injustice, betrayal, helplessness, or being misunderstood.

These behaviors can show up as complete disengagement from the situation or as feelings of justified retaliation: your old flight or fight response. Often, in hindsight you will notice you have been triggered, declaring, "Why did I do that? I know better than that!"

Your triggers were usually formed in your childhood and reinforced over time, resulting in a chain of automatic, uncontrollable projections and reactions. When the triggers are neutralized, there is a new freedom to make wiser choices in the midst of difficult situations. The energy that is liberated from the old pattern can then be used to intentionally create your desired results. That means you can focus on being happy and enjoying life because you aren't always being distracted by problems and upsets.

It also means you have a new freedom to evolve. No longer are you going around and around, trying to learn the same old lesson over and over again. You are free to continue on the fascinating path of spiritual discovery that will bring you to the ultimate prize, the living knowledge that you are one with the divine reality.

Making New Interpretations and Choices

Doing energy work makes it easier to make new choices, but it does not guarantee that you will. It is important to replace your old way of thinking with beliefs and choices that will take you to the future you desire. You can intentionally choose specific beliefs to create desirable results in your life.

What you focus on expands in your awareness. If you focus on new and powerful choices, you will magnetize yourself to attract new situations and people who match up with your purposefully created beliefs, attitudes, and anticipations.

Your *thoughts* become *beliefs* that become *feelings* that become *attitudes* that determine how you are going to *interpret* and *respond* to situations. Usually the interpretation is automatic and unconscious, but once you have trained yourself to observe your thoughts and identify your belief structures, you can modify your interpretations. Your interpretations are not beyond your command. As you take charge of your interpretations now, you begin to move to greater levels of authentic personal responsibility and power.

Your interpretations of your experiences determine the possibilities that are open or closed to you. If your interpretation is "I can succeed in the face of any obstacle," you will look for new solutions, ask new questions, ask for help and get it. If your interpretation is "No matter what I do, I always fail," you will see only that limited possibility. This perception rarely inspires positive action.

So here is the new game plan. Start tuning in to the higher-self perspective in every situation and acting as if this perspective is the most valid. You must continue to ask yourself, *What is the most empowering point of view about this situation?* or *What interpretation will take me to the future I desire?*

Sometimes it feels like a game of pretend, but the more you act as if the truth is true, the more you feel it to be true. You will be making a conscious effort to make new meanings and a conscious effort to behave differently. The more you make new choices and take new actions, the more your reality will become what you want it to be.

"

I hate making sales calls. It seems like a necessary evil in my business. It would be easier if I could hire someone to do it, but I can't afford it. I've been living with this dread and resistance for years, and I never knew I had a solution right under my nose. My wife and I have been using the CURE for about eight months, and it works great every time we use it. It never occurred to me I could use the process with an upset that wasn't about another person. My upset was with myself for not doing what I need to do to be successful in my business.

I decided to see what might be revealed if I used the CURE on this situation. Man, what a surprise! My bottom-line thought was I'll die because I can't do what I need to do. I never would have come up with that on my own in a million years. But that explains the near-panic feeling I have had to suppress just to pick up the phone. It always felt much stronger than simply fear of rejection. Now I know why.

I saw that this feeling came from an experience of being in the hospital when I was twelve years old. I was in a cast and traction, so I couldn't move around, and I was trying to buzz the nurse with the button by my pillow. It was late at night, and I was all alone and needed help for the pain. I kept pushing the button, but no one came, and I went into a panic, feeling afraid I was going to die. I wasn't going to die and I wasn't in danger, but I sure felt like it.

The CURE helped me see that the level of upset I was having about sales calls stemmed from this experience in the hospital. It still amazes me how things get so weirdly connected. But when doing the exercise, when I asked the question, "When is the earliest you remember feeling this way?" it was as plain as could be.

As soon as I could see what was really going on, I knew what to tap on with EFT. I can't say that I'm wild about making sales calls; there are still a whole lot of things I would rather do, but I can make them without the overwhelming resistance I used to feel. It is much easier for me to focus on *the value I offer in a sales conversation rather than the fear that I won't be able to get what I need.*

〉〉

Belief-Change Work

One of the most direct methods for permanently changing your interpretations is belief-change work. Using affirmations is an effective tool for belief-change work. Affirmations are positive thoughts on which you focus in specific ways to produce a desired result.

Your bottom-line thought is a thought you have about yourself that is out of harmony with your divine nature. If the problem is a thought about yourself that is *out of harmony* with your true nature, the solution, the cure, the antidote is a thought about yourself that is *in harmony* with your true nature.

A good affirmation, therefore, is a thought about yourself that is in alignment with your true, divine nature. Though it may be a part of your divine nature you are not yet experiencing, you can use affirmations to bring forth a latent, undiscovered part of you. Affirmations are like catalysts that activate a deeper part of your true nature.

If you discover that your bottom-line thought is *I can't get what I need*, an appropriate affirmation would be *I can have what I need*. Or if your bottom-line thought is *I'll be alone*, an appropriate affirmation would be something like *I am lovingly connected to others and I choose to feel it*. The method is essentially to state the opposite of the negative belief.

Using Affirmations Correctly

Affirmations have been greatly misunderstood and, we believe, misused. The key to using affirmations correctly is repetition or immersion into the new belief and linking the new belief with appropriate action and follow-through.

Merely posting an affirmation on your bathroom mirror or refrigerator is inadequate. If you compare the amount of time that you have been reinforcing your negative or limited belief with the microsecond that you spend occasionally glancing at your reminder note, you can see the former is much greater and therefore has greater force. For an affirmation to be effective, you must use the amplified power of your intention and consistent focus to break through the energy field that has been created by your past experiences. Your focus and intention gather enough momentum for you to pierce through the invisible membrane that has kept you locked in the past.

If you uncover a belief that says you can't get your needs satisfied because you are unworthy, an appropriate affirmation might be *I deserve to have all my needs satisfied. I am a good and lovable person.* But it is also important for you to follow through with attitudes of love and self-acceptance. It is also helpful to give to others the love and acceptance you want to receive. **Constantly chanting your affirmation in the absence of appropriate action only reinforces your feeling of limitation.**

Follow through with attitudes of love and self-acceptance.

An affirmation affirms the part of you that is not yet expressed and brings it into being. But sometimes people have resistance to working with affirmations. They just can't imagine well enough that they are true. Sometimes affirmations just feel like a great big lie.

In those cases, making new choice statements is a better way to go. The bottom-line thought, *I can't get what I need*, is transformed through the use of a statement which says, *I choose to know I can get what I need by making clear requests*. Or the bottom-line thought, *I'll be alone*, is resolved by focusing on a thought that says, *I choose to know I can be connected with others by expressing my love to them*. If your bottom-line thought is *I am a failure*, your choice statement could be, *Even though I have failed in the past, I choose to know I am free to succeed now*.

This method is essentially to say, "Even though _____ (fill in the negative), I choose to know _____ (fill in the positive)."

The key is repetition and intention. You can write, listen to, or say your affirmations. There are also specific energy techniques in Relationship Energy Repatterning that can be used with your affirmations to accelerate the integration.

Writing

Write your affirmation ten times in each person (first, second, and third person) every day:

I, (your name), now love and accept myself just as I am.

You, (your name), now love and accept yourself just as you are.

(Your name) now loves and accept himself/herself just as he/she is.

You can type them or write them in a notebook. The key is to use a high level of enthusiasm or determination. Rote repetition will not be effective. Do it like you really mean it.

Recording Cassette Tapes

Putting your affirmations on cassette tapes is effective for many people. Select your favorite affirmations and record them. Leave enough silence after every affirmation so that you can repeat it, either in your own mind or out loud. Repeat the affirmations over and over until your tape is about fifteen minutes long.

You can play your tape while you are getting ready in the morning or going to sleep at night. You can play it in the car while driving to work. Be creative. We know one person who used his commute time on the train to work with his affirmations. It's a much better use of time than reading the newspaper.

Saying Them Out Loud

You can make a game of saying your affirmations out loud while you are exercising. You can make up little melodies and sing them to yourself. Create a little ditty with one of your affirmations and sing it while you are on the treadmill or riding your bike or jogging. Maybe you will feel silly at first, but get over it. You can always hum them under your breath if a stranger approaches.

Using Reminder Cards

You can write your new choices on reminder cards (three-by-five index cards are perfect) and keep them at your desk or in your personal organizer. Occasionally pick them up and read through them, leaving a different card on display when you put them back.

Be creative and have some fun with it. Find new ways of reminding yourself. Leave notes for yourself in your coat pocket; put them in your socks. You can put them up as screen savers on your computer.

Affirming Heart to Heart Talks

In our book, *Straight from the Heart,* we teach a communication technique called Heart to Heart Talks^{SM}. There are four different kinds, and one of them is Affirming Heart to Heart Talks. In this book you can learn how to use affirmations in a spoken exercise with other people. When you use affirmations with another person, it amplifies their power.

You may buy this book, which also includes three audio classes that demonstrate Heart to Heart Talks, through our website. Go to www.EnlightenedPartners.com/bookstore.html, and you will be guided in downloading this valuable resource onto your own computer.

Imagine the difference between repeating to yourself the affirmation *I am a beautiful and lovable person; I deserve to be loved,* and looking into the eyes of someone you love and respect and hearing him or her tell you, "You are a beautiful and lovable person. You deserve to be loved and appreciated." Working with affirmations with other people accelerates the integration of the new beliefs into your mental-emotional structure.

The CURE in Action

Sharon and Jessie had been married for eight years. They had a comfortable life, both working out of their home in the country.

Occasionally Jessie would travel out of state for business. Sometimes he took Sharon with him, and sometimes he didn't.

One evening while Jessie was out of town Sharon started having flashes of intuition that Jessie was "involved" with one of his female business associates called Brenda. She tried to put the images out of her mind, but they were persistent and increasingly unpleasant. So she decided to call Jessie to settle her mind. She called him on his cell phone. As it turns out, he was at Brenda's house when he answered the call.

They chatted for a while as the knot in Sharon's stomach kept getting tighter and tighter. Before she even thought about it she heard herself blurt out, "Are you having an affair with Brenda?"

There was a long pause. "What are you talking about?" he said. "That's ridiculous!"

Sharon had never had these suspicions before, and she felt bad about doubting her husband's faithfulness. She quickly apologized and agreed she was "just being silly."

But the impressions in her mind just wouldn't go away. After calling a couple of girlfriends to distract her, she decided to call Jessie back. When he answered the phone his voice sounded "weird." Sharon started, "I don't know what to say, but I just can't let this go."

Jessie was silent for a long time. Sharon put her hand on her stomach as the dread started rising into her chest. "We'll talk about this when I get home," said Jessie.

"We will not. We'll talk about it right now." Sharon was dimly aware that a hysterical tone was spiking in her voice.

"We can't work this out over the phone, Sharon."

"You tell me right now. Have you slept with her?"

Jessie was trying to be calm, but he didn't know what to do. He was caught and lying more was only going to make things worse.

"Yes." He sat there on the couch in his lover's living room, paralyzed. The inescapable truth descended upon him. His wife knew. She was terribly hurt, he couldn't make this go away, and he didn't know what to do about it.

Sharon sat on the couch in the living room of the house she shared with her husband. She heard herself say, "You son of a bitch," and then the click of the phone as she slowly put it down. She sat there numb for quite a while. Then a banshee from hell erupted from her and laid waste to the living room.

After a series of volatile, back and forth conversations, they decided to see if they could schedule a session with us right away. They had both taken some classes from us and done some personal coaching with us before they had gotten married, and they had stayed in touch over the years. Sharon made the arrangements and let us know she would be flying in from Colorado for the session and Jessie would be driving down from Santa Barbara.

When they arrived separately at our front door it was the first time they had seen each other since the whole episode had begun. We opened the door. They both stood there, she livid, him oozing with guilt. We had some pretty difficult emotional terrain to cover, so we went straight to work.

In our consultation room we have two five-foot couches facing each other. Sharon and Jessie sat at the far ends of their couches, putting as much distance between them as they could. The emotional tension was excruciating. Often when we work with partnerships we will work privately with the individuals. We quickly moved into separate work areas. Sharon followed Paul into his private office.

We know that all challenges and upsets in a relationship are a co-creation. Upsets are learning opportunities, so the first thing we set out to do was to relieve the emotional intensity so they could begin to think more clearly and start to sort through how all of this came to be.

We can't tell you how many times we have thanked God for the relationship energy tools we use. They work quickly and gently to produce what would be considered miraculous results by any other standards. Within an hour, both Sharon and Jessie had cleared the majority of their emotional distress and had seen how their personal issues had dovetailed to create this heart-wrenching situation.

Neither of them was all the way through it, but they could both take responsibility for their own feelings, and that was the most important step. Blame is one of the most toxic emotions, and it undermines the rebuilding of trust. With both of their insights about their own issues firmly in mind, we embarked on the next leg of our journey, the healing and reconciliation of their relationship. We all sat down to talk about it.

As we facilitated their dialogue, it was fairly easy for each of them to discuss how they had participated in having the "event" occur. When people know how to take responsibility for their relationships without falling prey to the temptation of the victim role, they are able to take the most grievous situation and turn it around to their evolutionary advantage.

After they both revealed their individual "consciousness factors" we talked about a strategy to tackle what each of them had to work on within themselves and some new behaviors for the relationship itself. Insight in and of itself does little to transform negative consciousness factors. If you don't follow through with effective change methods, you are usually doomed to repeat the error in another form. The pain was so intense for both of them they were very motivated to do whatever they had to do to avoid this kind of thing again. They committed to their strategies and asked us to hold them accountable just in case this "miracle" didn't hold.

As it turned out, the event was a turning point in their marriage. They used it to learn and to grow closer together. They had several more waves of feeling to move through, but because they both took our Relationships Energy Repatterning Training they were able to move through it rather quickly and easily. They were able to support one another instead of getting stuck in a quagmire of overwhelming thoughts and feelings.

They stopped taking their relationship for granted and started investing more passion and creativity into it. It has paid off. They both say they are happier than they have ever been.

Mining the Gold

Through the alchemy of energy interventions you can transform mental-emotional blocks into wisdom and power. Using the CURE is a great way to continue sleuthing through the deep, dark corridors of your subconscious mind, discovering the negative mental-emotional structures that are buried there. But to mine the spiritual gold you must learn to transform these limiting ideas that carry so much emotional force.

This requires your focused intention. The process can seem challenging, especially if you are doing it all by yourself. Sharing the CURE with the people who are important to you can generate compatriots who will join you in this deep and powerful work.

Perhaps it is a buddy system where you meet for coffee and share your progress. Some people form support groups for just this purpose. If you feel you want support, create it. Ask others to help. Everyone will benefit from participating in this.

By controlling what is really within your power—how you interpret and respond to the world—you channel your energies to creation rather than reaction. By adopting radical personal responsibility, you explore the choices you do have, rather than succumbing to life-numbing helplessness. In the realm of human relationships, exercising this level of choice is tantamount to your spiritual elevation and evolution.

Take charge of your interpretations. Do your belief-change work. Make new choices and experiment with new behaviors. You will very quickly move along the path of your own journey to the best and highest in you.

Beyond the Mind: Connecting With Your Spiritual Essence

It is critical that you have a method for connecting with your spiritual essence on a regular basis. There are no words and no teaching that can provide you the *experience* or the awareness of who you are as a spiritual being. The words can point in the right direction, but they are not enough to bring you to the place of "arrival," the arrival of you knowing you are at one with the astonishing spiritual energy that is creating and sustaining the universe. It is your direct connection with this vast resource that will help you remain calm and resourceful, even in the face of hardship, loss, or danger.

You will need to discover for yourself what practices give you access to your spiritual nature. There are various forms of meditation, spiritual teachings, and communities for you to explore. Some people connect with the divine through body movement, dance, or music and art. We recently met someone who accesses her true self when she is spinning yarn; it never fails to put her in a deep meditative state. There are many different paths to the divine. You get to discover which ones work for you. Once you find them, work them. Participate in them regularly. The more frequent, usually the faster your progress.

Working with your mind can take you far on your healing journey, but when all the mind work is done, you may still feel that something is missing. You can be left with a deep disappointment, a yearning sense that life should be more than you have discovered so far. We have observed countless times the imbalance that occurs when people don't do their spiritual work in tandem with clearing the mental-emotional structures held in the subconscious mind.

It's All a Matter of Balance

If you focus for too long on the limitations held within your mind you start to over-identify with your pain, your story, your psychological "case." You can get hooked on "processing" your painful childhood and not notice that you are stuck in a self-created loop, recycling old material over and over again. This happens especially when you get a lot of love, support, or positive reinforcement for doing your healing work, or "feeling your feelings." The fear is that if you stop "processing" you will lose the love, praise, and attention. You don't seem to get the "lift-off" necessary to move you from self-absorption to self-realization.

On the other hand, if you retreat into meditation and use it as an anesthetic, you can end up dissociating yourself from the valuable learning opportunities of life; you can become an ungrounded "space cadet." If you use meditation as a way of avoiding your "lower nature," you never do the necessary work to transform it and you find your life does little to reflect the glory of the divine. You can feel the bliss from time to time, but you can't do anything worthwhile in the world to save your life. While you sit on your meditation cushion, you can feel a transcendent love pulsing through you, but as soon as you look into the eyes of someone who is disappointed in you, it vanishes. You can fill your mind with spiritual ideas but remain disconnected from the authentic power to realize them. This often leads to what we call the *spiritualized ego*. You can talk the talk, but you can't walk the walk. Your idealism will ultimately bring you pain because of your inability to integrate these transcendent ideas into the fabric of your life.

True spiritual practice means you work on both aspects simultaneously. You will find that the clearing work allows your mountaintop epiphanies to translate into authentic spiritual action in the marketplace and in your most intimate relationships.

The model of consciousness on the next page represents three aspects of mind: conscious mind, super-conscious mind, and subconscious mind. The conscious mind is aware of only a fraction of the incoming stimuli that constantly bombard our nervous system. Just as two thirds of an iceberg is submerged, most of what goes on in the mind is beyond conscious awareness.

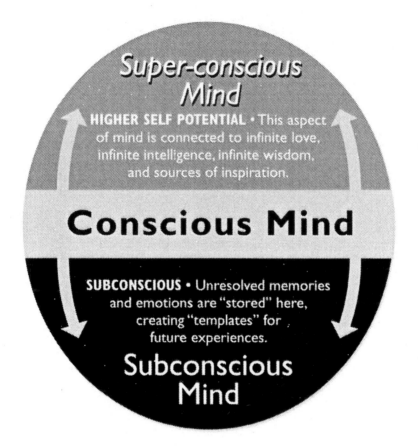

Super-conscious awareness is the domain of your higher self that is connected to infinite love, wisdom, and intelligence. The subconscious mind is the repository of memories and unresolved emotions. True transformational work requires expanding conscious awareness in both directions: healing unresolved issues from the past for the sake of *authentic spiritual presence* via the super-conscious mind, which is your own true, spiritual self.

As you do your deep inner work, letting go of beliefs and perceptions that no longer serve you, you will find yourself standing on a new and sparkling shore with an empty bucket in your hand. Who knows what wondrous new discoveries and experiences lie before you? Perhaps you will find that it is your own glorious spiritual nature, seeing with your eyes, speaking with your voice, and loving with your heart.

The **CURE**, Part Two: The Dialogue

BASED ON A FABLE TOLD IN INDIA
MANY YEARS AGO:

It was six men of Indostan,
To learning much inclined,
Who went to see the Elephant
(Though all of them were blind),
That each by observation
Might satisfy his mind.

The First approached the Elephant,
And happening to fall
Against his broad and sturdy side,
At once began to bawl:
"God bless me! but the Elephant
Is very like a wall!"

The Second, feeling of the tusk,
Cried, "Ho! what have we here
So very round and
smooth and sharp?
To me 'tis mighty clear
This wonder of an Elephant
Is very like a spear!"

The Third approached the animal,
And happening to take
The squirming trunk
within his hands,
Thus boldly up and spake:

"I see," quoth he, "the Elephant
Is very like a snake!"

The Fourth reached out
an eager hand,
And felt about the knee.
"What most this wondrous
beast is like
Is mighty plain," quoth he;
" 'Tis clear enough the Elephant
Is very like a tree!"

The Fifth, who chanced
to touch the ear,
Said: "E'en the blindest man
Can tell what this resembles most;
Deny the fact, who can?
This marvel of an Elephant
Is very like a fan!"

The Sixth no sooner had begun
About the beast to grope,
Than, seizing on the swinging tail
That fell within his scope,
"I see," quoth he, "the Elephant
Is very like a rope!"

And so these men of Indostan
Disputed loud and long,
Each in his own opinion
Exceeding stiff and strong,
Though each was partly in the right,
And all were in the wrong!

Moral:
So oft in theologic wars,
The disputants, I ween,
Rail on in utter ignorance
Of what each other mean,
And prate about an Elephant
Not one of them has seen!

Now that the CURE's Part One has given you some new insight into your upset, you are aware of your responsibility and have probably diminished the emotional charge. You are now ready for Part Two, The Dialogue.

Truth is Love's Doorway

In our book, *Straight From the Heart,* we say that truth is love's doorway. In other words, when we are honest and open about our true thoughts and feelings, it creates an environment in which love and affinity can flourish. One of the things we have found in our work over the years is that very often the things that partners cannot or will not talk about end up destroying the relationship.

It is important not only to be honest in your relationships, but also to be the kind of person with whom it is safe to be honest. If you get angry and upset whenever someone tells you something you don't like to hear, pretty soon they get the message that it is not safe to be honest with you.

Speaking your truth and listening to the truth of others is not always an easy thing to do. It is not always easy to know how to deal with an unpleasant truth you might hear, or to deal with another's reaction to an unpleasant truth of yours. For this reason, among others, it is often easier to just hold back and tell people what you think they want to hear. The only problem with that is that it doesn't allow you to get vital information that could foster trust, intimacy, or creativity in the relationship.

When you invite the other person to "talk about it," be sure to let them know you have been thinking about the situation. And you would like it if both of you could learn from it and work it out so that both of you feel satisfied.

Be Curious About the Other Person's Point of View

Even if the other person doesn't have the benefit of knowing about the CURE, the conversation will go better because of your own self-reflection and awareness. Because you have done your inner work and you know your bottom-line thought, you will be more aware of how you might tend to be filtering the conversation or distorting it.

Remember that upsets are for learning. When you do your outer work with the other person involved, use the same attitude of curiosity that works so well for you when you do the inner work. Intend to learn about how they see things. Learn what feelings they have had. Learn what they want to do about it. In other words, put as much focus on learning about them as you do on revealing your slant on things.

Creating a Learning Conversation

Most upsets occur because of misperceptions and miscommunications. Upsets happen because people are using different and conflicting information on which to base their opinions. People usually do the best they can with the knowledge they have. You both probably have different perceptions, feelings, identity concerns, beliefs, attitudes, and histories that have contributed to the upset. Unless you share this information with one another, you will rarely be able to get on the same page with each other. It will always feel "off" in some way when you try to relate.

In the learning conversation, you sort through the differences and use the information to learn about one another, exploring how you have both participated in a way that produced the upset. You use this information to avoid a similar upset in the future and to build a deeper level of understanding and affinity in your relationship. It is crucial for you to be as interested in hearing from them as you are in telling your side of things.

It is always helpful to voice your intention for the dialogue, because your intention greatly determines the quality of your exchange. If your intention is to make them wrong or punish them for what you feel they "did to you," they are going to feel that, no matter what else you might say. Make sure you truly intend to generate a learning conversation; don't just pay it lip service.

You might begin the conversation saying something like, "Our relationship is important to me, and I want to do what I can to clear up any misunderstanding that has happened between us," or "I want us to be able to resolve this upset so we both learn from it and can have an even better relationship," or something along these lines.

Intend to generate a learning conversation.

When there has been an upset and you haven't talked about it with them yet, you can expect there will be emotional undercurrents. This makes it a difficult conversation. In their book *Difficult Conversations*, Douglas Stone, Bruce Patton, and Sheila Heen of the Harvard Negotiation Project discuss how every difficult conversation has three separate conversations happening simultaneously. They collapse into one another and appear as one, but they aren't. If you can be aware of these different levels of conversation and tease them apart, things will go more smoothly. These different conversations have to do with perceptions, feelings, and identity issues.

This certainly has been our experience in facilitating learning conversations. In our view, the four most important pieces in a learning conversation are perceptions, feelings, identity concerns, and personal responsibility.

The Perception Conversation has to do with sorting through one another's different views on the same issue. It is important to avoid arguing about whose truth is more valid than the other. Let it be okay that you remember things differently. Simply be curious about how they see it without playing a right/wrong game.

The Feelings Conversation is delicate and potentially volatile. If everyone's true feelings aren't acknowledged, they tend to leak out into the conversation in the form of misperceptions. We cannot emphasize enough the importance of dealing with feelings openly, honestly, in safe and appropriate ways.

Creating a safe climate for all parties to engage in the feelings conversation is an art well worth learning. There are specific dos and don'ts, detailed below, which make this emotional minefield much easier to navigate.

It is very important to listen to someone talk about their feelings without interrupting them in any way and, most important, not to judge or invalidate those feelings, even when they seem unwarranted to you. This can be a real challenge when those feelings appear to put you in a bad light. But if you are aware of your own filters, you will not take it all so personally.

The Identity Conversation highlights how the issue and the way it is being dealt with impact the identity of each participant. The question "What does this mean about me?" is lurking just below the conscious level of awareness, and both your minds are tending to leap to all kinds of conclusions. Often, both parties are concerned that their identity will be painfully impacted. Be sensitive to how the upset may be affecting their sense of self in ways of which they may be unaware.

The Personal Responsibility Conversation is extremely important in transmuting any blame or ill will. In the absence of personal responsibility, all you can do is point fingers. As you have learned before, personal responsibility is a skill. You and the other person may bring different levels of this skill to the conversation. It is important that you allow for this difference without pressuring the other to match your skill level. You can model a high level of skill and inspire another, but it is counterproductive to try and teach them personal responsibility until the upset is completely resolved. It is so easy for people to misinterpret your "help" as controlling or patronizing.

Guard against using personal responsibility either as a shield or a weapon. For some, the temptation may be to react defensively: "I'm not responsible for your feelings, so *you* go sort out your own stuff. I don't have anything going on, and I don't want to talk about it any more." For others, the temptation may be to go on the offensive, indulging in saying whatever they want, with whatever malicious momentum they may feel, because ultimately they bear no responsibility for other people's feelings.

Neither of these approaches fosters healing. Neither of them fosters cooperation, or caring, or love. They may abide by the letter of the law of radical personal responsibility, but they completely ignore its spirit. Instead, approach the dialogue with openness to hear and express what is in both your hearts, and to do so with the intention of creating connection. It is ideal if you can both interpret the upset as an opportunity to grow, seeing that once you understand each other better, you will probably have a better relationship because of it.

Getting Ready for the Dialogue

As you get ready for the dialogue it's important to remember that the other person may have access to different information than you have, which may have influenced what they've said or done. They may have feelings you might never imagine they have. Or they could be surprised to learn about your feelings or motivations. During the dialogue, both your interpretations may change as you exchange your different views. It is best if you have a conversation about your final interpretations about the upset.

Remember, a difficult conversation will go much better if you begin it with an attitude of curiosity rather than using it as a forum to state your own position.

Until now, you've probably done your best to avoid difficult conversations. Even when you knew how important it was to discuss a topic, you procrastinated and procrastinated, hoping against hope that somehow the problem would magically disappear by itself if you just waited long enough. Alas, this is one of the most significant errors people make in their relationships. You can make a situation worse by delaying important dialogues.

Begin with an attitude of curiosity.

The characteristics of enlightened conflict resolution are a direct, straightforward exchange of information and emotional authenticity. Dropping your mask and being emotionally honest can sometimes leave you feeling vulnerable, but that is just the reason it can be so disarming. Mutual vulnerability communicates a willingness to trust and be trusted, to care and be cared for.

The needed honesty can be compromised by emotional incongruence: conflict between what a person says and what a person feels. Most people have learned to hide their true feelings, either to protect themselves or to manipulate others, so creating this new level of honesty can be challenging.

Sometimes you're aware of your own incongruence, and sometimes you aren't. Sometimes you may intentionally lie about your feelings to get the upper hand or play it safe. Hiding your feelings on purpose is almost always a self-defeating move because it is so transparent; ninety-nine percent of the time, the tension in your facial muscles reveals what you are trying to cover up. People may not always notice it right away, but after they leave the situation and have some time to reflect on it, it usually dawns on them. They may not confront you about it because it is not worth the effort. They will feel wary and simply "go polite" but keep their distance.

Hiding your feelings on purpose is almost always a self-defeating move.

At other times, you may be out of touch with your feelings (numb) or trying to fool yourself into maintaining a particular self-image. Perhaps it is an image of being nice or spiritual or in control. But just beneath the surface, your fear of looking bad, or being wrong, or being cast aside dictates your defensiveness. Defensiveness is almost always interpreted by others as aggression, which escalates arguments. You may think you are communicating clearly but you are really sending mixed messages.

By definition, mixed messages are confusing. They can be crazy-making and infuriating. They undermine trust and usually make conflict resolution a difficult proposition. This is one of the most important reasons to do your "inner work" before you have your dialogue. If you are still feeling angry or blaming but mouthing words of reconciliation or good intent, you will be incongruent.

Our bodies are strands in the web of a subtle communication system in the universe. Our ability to sense invisible messages is hardwired into us as part of our survival mechanism. Despite this innate gift, many people can't even sense their own feelings anymore, and their ability to read these subtle signals can be diminished. But we can relearn to tune in to these energies and notice all manner of things that most people don't. We can tune into the invisible but palpable signals that allow us to read our own emotions and those of others.

The words of a conversation are transmitted on an invisible carrier wave of emotion. The emotion is more powerful than the words alone. In other words, the emotion is louder. Sometimes the emotion is screaming so loudly you can't even hear the words being said. Consequently, one of the worst things you can do is lie about your feelings or try to hide them. All it does is send mixed messages and makes others feel like they are standing on shaky ground, causing all manner of silent alarms and red alert signals to clamor through their energy field. There is a dreadful, unsettling feeling that comes with that "everything looks okay, so why does it feel so bad, and where is the danger really coming from?" feeling that usually throbs in the stomach and raises the hackles.

Have you ever gotten a mixed message? Someone says, "It's no big deal," but you can tell from the voice tone they are quite upset. Perhaps they are saying, "I just want us to be friends," but you feel like they want to make you wrong for a little while first. They may be pretending like they *want* to be supportive but they are *acting* like you need a lesson, and they are just the one to give it to you, with a little bit of punishment to make the point. We have often seen people cloak their hostility behind lofty phrases of "making peace" or creating a "win-win outcome," but they would just as soon eat someone's heart out if it doesn't go their way.

Just as it is easy to tell when someone else is being emotionally incongruent, it can be quite difficult to notice when you are being emotionally incongruent. It can be extremely difficult for people who place a high value on peace or kindness to be honest with themselves (or anyone else for that matter) about their darker emotions. It can generate a deep inner conflict to have angry feelings when you see yourself as a nice person. If you have been a victim of emotional violence, it can be even more difficult. It can feel as though your survival or your dignity depends on how deftly you can stuff your feelings.

It can generate a deep inner conflict to have angry feelings when you see yourself as a nice person.

Over time, people automatically suppress feelings they judge to be bad. This leads to acute emotional incongruence. What can be so crazy-making is you can't feel the feelings you are transmitting to others. If you want to learn to be emotionally congruent, it is vital that you recognize the importance of learning to feel safe with all of your emotions. Look to see the role fear or anger has played in your life. As you practice the CURE, you will learn to be more honest with yourself about your inner world, and it will become easier to be honest with others.

There is a distinction between being honest about your feelings and acting them out. We are not advocating that you go around huffing and puffing, slamming your fist on tables, trembling underneath the conference table or sobbing at office meetings. Simply acknowledging your feeling state (such as by saying, "I am angry at how this has been handled so far, but I would like to work this out,") can neutralize the negative effects of emotional incongruence. It will inspire people's trust. Acting out your feelings more often alienates people.

The truth is that emotional dishonesty has no place in conscious conflict resolution. If you aren't willing to be honest, you are not ready for Part Two, the dialogue. A robust vulnerability is required. If you are still feeling hurt or blaming or angry, the best thing is to be honest about it. You don't want to mess things up by pretending otherwise. Remember, emotional authenticity is disarming. If you are afraid, simply acknowledging your anxiety can neutralize any emotional incongruence. If it still seems they *are to blame*, you can say something like this: "A part of me still wants to blame you while another part of me wants to be responsible for myself." If you are still angry, you can say, "I'm still angry but I want to let go of it." The honest, direct approach in the learning conversation is usually the best way to go.

If you aren't willing to be honest, you are not ready for Part Two, the dialogue.

The hallmark of a strong and healthy relationship is direct, compassionate, and honest communication, especially about difficult subjects. Lay your cards on the table, speak from the heart, honor one another's perspective, and discover real solutions that serve everyone involved. Most people would like to be able to do that all the time, yet the fear of things not turning out keeps them from even trying.

Relationships are important, and none of us wants to make a difficult situation worse by saying the wrong thing.

The fact of the matter is, difficult conversations are a part of life, and avoiding them is not a real solution. The solution is learning to master them so they are less difficult. This skill will affect the way you feel about yourself in a very positive way and give you the confidence to create and maintain truly healthy relationships.

Guidelines Can Set the Mood

Often people have wildly different attitudes about resolving conflict. Many people have a win-or-lose point of view that can sabotage a learning conversation. We have found it extremely helpful to establish "new rules for the game" to set the mood for a learning conversation.

Using the following guidelines for Part Two of the CURE will make your dialogue easier and more rewarding. One of the most important things to understand about communication is that **your intention determines your results.** These guidelines are to declare the most positive, supportive intention possible for the dialogue.

Guidelines for the Dialogue

1. I will communicate with the intention of producing more harmony and understanding in the relationship.

2. I will participate in a spirit of goodwill, being as honest as I can be.

3. I am committed to a mutually beneficial outcome, recognizing that if one of us loses, the whole relationship loses.

4. I intend to take responsibility for my own experience, knowing it reflects my personal thoughts, beliefs, feelings, and attitudes.

5. I intend to use any mistakes as a learning opportunity, and I will practice a forgiving attitude.

6. I will continue to communicate until we find a resolution that works for everyone involved.

7. I will use the situation to learn about myself and to become a better person.

8. I will keep this conversation confidential and not talk about it with others, unless we both agree otherwise.

The Eight Steps to Mutual Understanding and Resolution

The first four steps are focused on learning and discovery, putting your different pieces of the jigsaw puzzle together. The last four steps are about rebuilding trust, clarity, and coordinating action for the future.

Step 1. Perception Conversation. Take turns sharing your perceptions about the situation. Remember not to argue about whose perception is more valid. Listen deeply to the other person. Don't listen to the voice inside your head that may be commenting on what they say. Remember, it is okay that you see or remember things differently.

Step 2. Feelings Conversation. Take turns sharing the feelings you have each had about this situation. Be responsible for your feelings and avoid blaming the other person for what you feel. Remember just to listen from the heart without judging, being a compassionate witness to their point of view. Do your best to listen without judgment.

Step 3. *Identity Concerns.* Bring in the Identity Conversation. With a curious attitude, ask, "Is there any way that our individual sense of self has been affected in this situation?" Take turns listening to one another.

Step 4. *Personal Responsibility.* The first most important move for you to make in this situation is for you to take responsibility for your part without requiring that they take responsibility for theirs. People have different levels of expertise in taking responsibility.

If you both know how to practice the CURE, and you have completed the worksheet, you may want to refer to your worksheets to include anything else that might shed some light on the situation for the other person.

Usually, you won't want to include the thoughts and feelings you were venting at the beginning of the worksheet. Most of the time it is not helpful.

Typically, the more people share, the greater the learning opportunity is for everyone concerned. So if you feel it is appropriate, you can share the beliefs and attitudes you have that could have contributed to the upset.

Step 5. Apologies. Make whatever apologies are appropriate. There is a tremendous healing power in an apology. Some people resist making an apology because they mistakenly think it is admitting wrongdoing. But apologizing for the distress in the situation and whatever you may have done to contribute to it goes a long way to restoring harmony. Try it on for size: "I apologize for whatever I may have done to upset you." (See? It hardly hurt at all.)

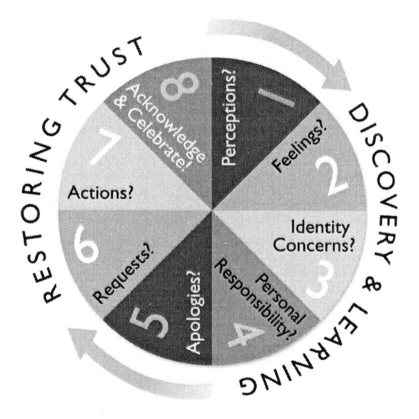

Step 6. Requests. Make any requests of one another that will further cooperation in your future together. You are each responsible for your own needs being met, and one of the best ways to do that is

by making clear requests that inspire cooperation, rather than demanding compliance.

You can both discuss any ideas you have about what needs to happen for this upset to be completely resolved so that you both feel good about the whole thing. Ask each other, "What needs to happen, if anything, for you to feel resolved about this upset?" You are establishing mutual goodwill for the future.

Step 7. Future Actions. Come to an agreement about how this kind of thing might be handled in the future. Are there any new strategies you need to put in place? See if there are any more steps that need to be taken, such as communicating with other people who may have been affected by the upset.

Step 8. Acknowledge and Celebrate. You may want to underscore what good came out of the upset. For example, "You know, I can see that this turned out okay. We understand one another better than before and that is a good thing."

or

"As we complete this conversation I see that the good that came from this difficult situation outweighs the bad. I've learned a lot about you and myself. I'm glad that together we were able to turn this around so that there are no remaining bad feelings. Thanks."

You can also acknowledge them for their willingness, curious attitude, giving you the benefit of the doubt, or risking that it might not work and trying anyway. Be as generous with one another as you can be.

Thank them for their time or their goodwill or whatever seems appropriate. This nurtures the relationship and acts as a healing salve for whatever remaining feelings of upset may linger.

Often the outcome from the dialogue is so positive people feel like celebrating. The affinity that has developed is so high, a mere acknowledgment and thank you seems inadequate. We encourage you to give in to this impulse to celebrate. It strengthens the relationship and brings in the perfect top note of joy.

Some of the most popular ideas for celebrating are nurturing experiences like sharing a cup of coffee or a cocktail or a meal together. Other pampering experiences are good for celebrating alone, like candlelight baths, listening to your favorite music, or indulging in one of your favorite pastimes.

When the Other Person Isn't Familiar With the CURE

When you are talking with someone who knows nothing about the CURE or personal responsibility, use this first approach. You simply intend to have a harmonious problem-solving conversation. It is best to have the conversation at a time when you will not be interrupted by anything or anyone else.

The inner work you did will probably allow you to navigate this conversation without getting triggered again, and you will find yourself much more resourceful because you have cleared your own issue. Your communication should be free of any emotional edge. You will be much more able to generate a harmonious and cooperative dialogue.

Because you know how to practice the CURE, it is likely you have more skill in non-adversarial conflict resolution. The burden of consciousness dictates that you will probably take the lead in the conversation; the art in this for you is leading without being controlling. One of the best ways to do this is to ask questions rather than give directives. For example, "Do you think it would be helpful if we share our different perceptions to start?" rather than, "I'd like you to tell me your side of the story, then we can talk about our feelings, and then . . . ".

It will be important for you to acknowledge your responsibility for the upset without expecting them to be able to do the same. You will invite them to share their perception, and you will offer yours. You will want to make it as safe for them to acknowledge their feelings as you can. You can speak lightly about some of your feelings; just be careful not to overdo it. You probably have a lot more insight into your whole "feelings" story than they do, and you don't need to give them all the information you have, just enough so they get a sense of how the upset has affected you. All the insights you gained from doing Part One may be more information than they need or want.

Your communication should be free of any emotional edge.

After you draw them out and they have revealed some of their perceptions and feelings, you may ask, "If there was anything we could learn from this situation, what do you think it might be?"

Or you can take the lead by setting an example. "I have found it helpful if I can turn difficult situations into learning opportunities and so I have asked myself the question, 'What can I learn about myself in this situation?' What I came up with is . . . Is there anything you think you could learn about yourself from all of this?" Accept whatever response they give, even if it is a resounding no.

After the learning opportunity has been clarified, you may want to make whatever apology you think would be helpful, then make any requests and ask if they have any. Discuss if there is anything else either of you could do to prevent this kind of thing happening in the future. Then thank them for taking the time to talk to you.

When You Both Know the CURE And Are in a More Formal Relationship

This next approach is to be used in a more formal relationship where you both know how to practice the CURE and you have both completed Part One, the inner work.

Perhaps the upset happened at work or with someone you meet from time to time in a group situation, like church or Little League. In this case, usually the quality of your relationship affects other people.

The fact that you aren't getting along or perhaps not even speaking to one another creates emotional undercurrents that other people can feel, which tends to be unpleasant for everyone. Sometimes it leaves mutual friends or associates feeling as if they have to make a choice between you.

Your conflict with each other can generate conflicting loyalties for others. Often unresolved upsets act as a divisive element in communities and families, souring the times when you are all together. With this second approach, you want to clear up the upset, but you don't necessarily feel the desire for a deep friendliness or a close, intimate relationship. You're looking to build trust so that you may enjoy authentic, cordial interactions.

Because you both have experience with the CURE, you won't have to take the lead. Perhaps you will want to use the diagram on page 159 to frame the conversation. You can almost use it as a checklist: "Okay, we've discussed the first three parts. Are we ready for number four?" You can include the identity concerns with this person. You probably wouldn't have included it in a conversation with someone who knew nothing about the CURE because "having identity concerns" is not something they would already understand.

You can share information you gained from doing Part One if you think it would be helpful, but you may want to edit the more personal information. After all, this is not a close relationship but a more formal one. You want to be careful not to overburden the relationship with too much information. It is a judgment call really. Every situation will be different. If you are paying attention to them as you talk, you will get some clues if you are going deeper than they are comfortable with.

For Your Closest Relationships

The third approach is for close relationships. This is a relationship in which you want to feel completely at ease. When you look into one another's eyes, you want to feel a heart connection. You want to feel like you really understand one another. You want to feel the freedom to be yourself, and you want them to feel completely free to be themselves without fear of judgment.

Perhaps this is a relationship where you sense there is an opportunity for the emergence of your spiritual nature, a place where together you can honor the shared evolutionary impulse of your souls. As fellow human beings you both live within a dynamic tension generated between the security impulse of your conditioned creature self and that soulful part of you that is driven to evolve and expand.

In this relationship you want to honor the adventurous, risk-taking, pushing-the-envelope self. You are both ready to step outside the safety zone and reveal yourselves to one another in complete vulnerability. You recognize an uncommon opportunity to experience spiritual truth together, and you are unwilling for any ego projections or misunderstandings to sully the highest possibilities. You want this relationship to be a loving relationship of magnificent depth, filled with safety, strength and truth.

In this relationship, you share the intimate details you have gained from Part One. You look to see how your learning opportunities have dovetailed. Perhaps you are both mirrors for one another. You may both be learning the same lesson. Perhaps you are learning it is safe to ask for what you want or it is safe to say no without fear of losing love or respect. Whatever the lessons may be, your disclosure to one another is done in a spirit of mutual support. You are partnering in one another's spiritual unfolding. There is a sacred aspect that is being honored with your conversation.

In the Unlikely Event the CURE Does Not Succeed

If you still feel distant from one another after the dialogue, we suggest you get a coach or someone else to facilitate a deeper level of resolution. Sometimes it just takes expert help to complete these things. Maybe you will want to do it together, or perhaps you will want to do it individually. From a spiritual perspective, it is worth whatever time or effort you need to bring to the situation.

Remember to check in with your higher spiritual values. Are they still the top priority in this relationship, or has another priority somehow slipped in without notice? Do your best to keep going for the highest spiritual thought and the truest expression of your divine nature!

Occasionally, using the CURE fails. Though the times have been few, they are still worth mentioning. It usually comes down to willingness or, rather, lack of it. Somehow, on one side or both, the willingness wanes. Often it is a lack of insight into the deeper emotional undercurrents or just plain fear to confront the deeper issue that has been triggered.

Sometimes people don't feel safe enough to go deeper, and it can take some time for the safety to develop. Sometimes, it is lack of a clear benefit for resolving the issue. One of the things we recommend if this happens for you is to discuss what it might be costing everyone involved if this situation doesn't get worked through.

Sometimes these issues bring you to the outer edge of your own evolutionary journey. You get to a place where you just don't know what to do. You reach the limit of your own wisdom and ability. We encourage you to use your spiritual resources. Pray, ask for guidance, and get some expert help.

CHAPTER SEVEN

Living With the **CURE**, or Not?

To put the world in order,
we must first put the nation in order.
To put the nation in order,
we must first put the family in order.
To put the family in order,
we must first cultivate our personal life.
To cultivate our personal life,
we must first set our hearts right.

CONFUCIUS

"

*My girlfriend introduced me to the CURE, and I believe it saved my
life. Because of what I learned doing it, I was finally able to leave an
abusive relationship.*

*I had left Ronnie so many times I lost count, but I always came back. I
loved him desperately, or at least I thought I did, and I couldn't let go of
him no matter how badly he hurt me. All my friends were fed up with me,
and they all told me I should leave him—that I deserved better—but I still
couldn't stop going back to him.*

*After a really bad fight when he hit me in the face, I was staying at my
girlfriend's house trying to decide what I was going to do. She pulled out
these papers and told me she wanted to do this process with me that she
thought would help.*

When she asked me, "What does it mean about you that Ronnie hits you?" my mind kept saying, "I'm bad. I don't deserve love." No matter how many times she asked the question it kept coming back to those two thoughts.

Then she asked me, "What does it mean about you that you're afraid you will keep letting Ronnie hurt you and your life won't be worth living?" That was my fear in the upset. My mind said, "I don't deserve love," then "there is something wrong with me," then "I should try harder," and then "if I try to be good, maybe I'll get some love."

We put the two different "bottom-line statements" into one. It read, "I don't deserve love, but if I try to be good, maybe I'll get love." After she wrote that down, I cried like a baby. After I finished, she asked me, "When is the earliest you can remember feeling this way?" Immediately I thought about my father. My dad was an alcoholic, and he would get very mean when he was drinking. I remember how Mom and all us kids would be very careful when he was drinking. We never knew what would set him off.

It was totally obvious to me that the feeling I had when my dad would get drunk and I would try so hard to be good and helpful was just like the feeling I had with Ronnie when he would get angry with me. When Ronnie would get moody, I always tried to "love him out of it." Most of the time it worked. But there were a lot of times it wouldn't, and he would get violent anyway.

Doing this CURE exercise gave me the first inkling that my relationship with Ronnie had a lot to do with my relationship with my dad. I don't know how to explain it, but doing the exercise gave me different eyes to see my relationship with Ronnie.

I wish I could say that I never went back to Ronnie again, except I did once more. But it was different that time. My "new eyes" helped me see how locked in I was to my painful childhood. And how my relationship with Ronnie just kept me there.

Slowly, it became clear to me that if I was ever going to be happy, I would have to leave him. It looked like just about everything he said reinforced the idea that I didn't deserve love or good treatment. And I was tired beyond tired of feeling that way.

After three months I left him, and I've never gone back. I know I still have some healing to do about my dad, and I want to do it even though the idea makes me nervous. I want to love myself more, and I want relationships that help me do that.

》》

The CURE, just like any other tool, works only if you use it. Using it is simply a matter of intention and having the tool at hand. One way is to make a master list of the thirteen questions from Part One and keep it for future reference. Or you can keep a blank CURE worksheet on your computer desktop. To download it from our website, go to www.EnlightenedPartners.com/thecureworksheet.pdf.

If you haven't done that yet, do it now. Then print out a master copy. Take it to the copy shop and make about twenty-five or thirty copies. Then stash them around your life—your briefcase, desk drawer, bedside table drawer, in your car, your office—all of the places you spend time. If it is handy, you are much more likely to use it. If it's not, you won't. It's as simple as that. The worst thing you can do is think this is a great idea and just leave your CURE worksheets somewhere that you can forget about them.

Beyond simply having worksheets close at hand for use whenever you need it, there are predictable challenges to using the CURE, and it is a good idea to know what they are in advance so you can recognize them when they occur.

Resistance to Change

One of the main challenges to using the CURE is resistance to change. Let's face it: The familiar is comforting, even if it isn't particularly good for you. It just seems to be a part of the human psychology that a part of us wants things to stay the same, even while another part of us complains about it.

However, in a rapidly changing world filled with ambiguity and uncertainty, we are required to change and evolve or perish. New skills for adaptability and flexibility are an evolutionary necessity. But if every change in life sparks a crisis of self-esteem because we are uncertain that we will be valued in the new order of things, we resist change. It is better if we can greet change with a happy heart, because change is here to stay and, as they say, resistance is futile.

Lack of Familiarity

One of the biggest hurdles to integrating this new conflict resolution technique is your lack of familiarity with it. It will take some time for you to learn it. You didn't grow up watching people resolve conflict in this way, and even if you know other people who use the technique, you probably don't get to watch them practicing it. You aren't watching it on the TV or hearing it on the radio. So, in the beginning, it can seem a bit awkward and unfamiliar.

It can be as if a voice in your head says, *Hey, my mom and dad didn't do it this way, so it must not be right for me.* Yet when we ask people in our seminars how many of them would want to have a relationship exactly like their parents' relationship, only one percent of the people raise their hand.

The point we are making here is that this new process hasn't been modeled for you, so in the beginning it may not *feel* natural. But in time, through repetition, it will come as naturally as breathing. The more you do it, the easier it becomes.

Fear of Making Mistakes

The third kind of resistance comes from the fear of making a mistake. Well, guess what: You will. But you will learn something every time you complete a CURE worksheet. You will learn from any mistakes you make, and in time you will become proficient—and much more quickly than you might think. Please give yourself permission to make mistakes, and don't let the fear stop you. Upsets are part of the human condition, and you can keep handling them the way you always have, or you can learn a new, more effective way. Making mistakes is part of the learning process.

Not Enough Time

The fourth challenge will be thinking you don't have time and that it takes too long. The truth about this is that you waste more time blaming and feeling like a victim if you don't find out how you are responsible for your own pain. It is more difficult to live in the pain of doing it the old way. The idea that it is "just too much trouble" is usually a smoke screen for some of the other resistances we have already mentioned.

No one is *that* busy. It is more an issue of priorities. If you can't find the time, it's because you don't *really* want to. The question is why it isn't more important to you or what the payoff is in keeping things the way they have been.

Sometimes it is simply a matter of emotional or intellectual laziness. The level of emotional and intellectual rigor applied to the CURE was not modeled for most of us. And so it is a new move, something extra we have to do. In an already busy life this "extra" can seem like too much.

Wanting to Be Right at All Costs

The fifth challenge is wanting to be right about your point of view and wanting the other person to be wrong. Needing to be right neutralizes your willingness to work things out. This kind of self-righteousness and stubborn pride will keep you stuck in power struggle. Have you ever heard of the saying, "Do you want to be right or do you want to be happy?" What we say is, "Do you want to be right or do you want to be wise?"

Without willingness, nothing works. So, like the rest of it, this one is up to you, too. No more blame, no more victim. You make your choices, and you get to live with them. And remember, you are never upset for the reason you think—and neither is anyone else. The magic of the CURE is that you get to see every time you think you are upset about one thing, it always turns out to be something else.

When it *really* looks like someone else has offended or hurt you in some way, you will see that the pain you are experiencing was there all along, just waiting to be triggered. **Only when you are able to look at and discuss the real causes of your upset can you experience genuine healing and resolution.**

Misidentifying With Your Painful Feelings

One of the most curious phenomena of the human mind is the attachment to pain. Recurrent emotional states have a powerful effect on your sense of self. You have come to know who you are by the way you feel. There can be a concern that you might not know who you are without your anger or anxiety or fear or sadness. If you weren't feeling those feelings, somehow it just "wouldn't feel right." The loss of the familiar state sometimes causes people to feel uneasy. One of our clients expressed it like this: "I don't feel right without the 'edge' my anxiety gives me. If I don't have a certain degree of anxiety, I'll drop my guard, and that would be dangerous." We have occasionally used Relationship Energy Repatterning to release people from limiting emotional states only for them to discover they want some of their negative emotions back because they are afraid they won't be effective without them.

It is as if they have gotten used to dancing with the same partner to the same music for so long that when they move to a new partner with a different beat, they feel as if they can't dance at all. The unfamiliar is too disorienting, so they start searching for what is familiar to reorient them. This deep, unconscious misidentification with pain can be so powerful as to prevent people from taking action to liberate themselves from their pain. Relief can be right in front of their nose, and they won't see it.

They can even get very angry if you try and help them to let go. They misperceive you as an enemy trying to take something valuable away from them. This phenomenon often accounts for people not using the CURE even when they know it will work for them.

If this happens to you, you will notice it as replaying the upset over and over again in your mind, re-telling yourself and others the "story" that justifies your feelings. With the CURE and Relationship Energy Repatterning ready to give you relief at a moment's notice and your stubborn refusal to take positive steps, the reason for your continuing to be upset is staring you right in the face. For some incomprehensible reason *you want to feel this way*, no matter how much it hurts or you complain about it. This level of egoic cunning can be a formidable obstacle.

Acknowledging this, if it applies, is one of the most important things you can do to move beyond it. Admitting that "sometimes I'm attached to my pain and I don't want to let it go, because I might not know who I am without it" tells a very deep level of truth. It is *the* truth that can set you free!

After this profound level of truth telling, you gain the power that comes from deep self-awareness. Your new ability to witness the part of you that is choosing pain liberates you from the self-deception that has kept you stuck.

After you do this for a while, you will feel the grip of the attachment start to loosen. Then you can begin to choose to discover who you are without these recurrent bouts of your own personal brand of pain.

Feeling Too Vulnerable

Personal responsibility takes courage. Becoming aware of your internal landscape can be painful sometimes. Looking deeply at the beliefs and feelings you have pushed into the dark corners of your subconscious mind is not always easy or comfortable. The beliefs you have that separate you from an ongoing experience of your spiritual nature are usually so uncomfortable and painful that you are in denial of their existence.

Using the CURE takes you right into the center of these old buried belief structures, and often you will feel vulnerable. It is as if you have removed your armor. You can feel "too vulnerable" even when you are completely safe. You may feel dangerously exposed as the memory that birthed the negative structure pours into your awareness. But the thing to remember is that the feeling is only temporary. The feeling is a memory washing through your awareness, on its way out.

People who care about you can make this process easier. Loved ones can remind you that confronting the truth of a situation makes you stronger in the long run. It enables you to remind yourself that these negative beliefs aren't the truth about you, even though they may feel true in the moment. The only way you can become familiar with the healing process is to choose it over and over again. Even when it feels scary. Even when you feel vulnerable. Even when you doubt that you can truly be healed.

Remind yourself that these negative beliefs aren't the truth about you.

The more experiences you have of awakening from your self-imposed denial, the easier it becomes to be truly honest with yourself. With an intention of self-acceptance and forgiveness you gain the strength necessary to observe your own thoughts, feelings, and attitudes. You gain a deepening awareness that nothing outside of you hurts you. The illusion that you have to defend yourself from the outer world starts to dissolve. And time and time again, you feel returned to your essential self.

The benefit of this over time is you feel safer and stronger. Through repetition, you learn it is safe for you to face your inner demons. You learn that when you do, you are always the victor. All this can be claimed through personal responsibility.

How Will Your Life Be Different?

It is important to imagine what your life will be like when it is more of an upset-free zone, because that is what will happen with the regular use of the CURE. Because you are addressing the cause of your upsets and not just the symptoms, the more you use it, the less your symptoms appear. That means fewer upsets.

You will become increasingly immune to the things that used to trigger you into anger, sadness, despair, depression, self-pity, projection, and blame. You will live in the experience of your true personal power to determine your experience of reality. People and events might push your buttons, but the reaction you feel will be increasingly diminished in intensity. Upsets will last for shorter and shorter periods. The times between upsetting episodes in your life will grow farther and farther apart.

We encourage you to introduce the CURE to the people in your life. The more people who practice enlightened conflict resolution with you, the more harmonious your relationships will be. You will be operating at a much higher level of trust, love, cooperation, and creativity in all relationships where you can practice the CURE.

Living in a World of Personal Responsibility

Albert Einstein once said,

> A human being is a part of a whole, called by us "Universe," a part limited in time and space. He experiences himself, his thoughts and feelings, as something separated from the rest—a kind of optical delusion of his consciousness. This delusion is a kind of prison for us,

restricting us to our personal desires and to affection for a few persons nearest to us. Our task must be to free ourselves from this prison by widening our circle of compassion to embrace all living creatures and the whole of nature in its beauty. Nobody is able to achieve this completely, but striving for such achievement is in itself a part of the liberation and a foundation for inner security.

The world of personal responsibility is a safer world. Rather than acting out and recycling our inner conflicts in relationship after relationship, we can claim a new peace forged out of our deep self-awareness. With this self- awareness, we gain wisdom. As we individually and collectively emerge from the tunnel of suffering created by misunderstandings and misperceptions, we can begin to heal. We can open our eyes and see a new world with new possibilities for getting along with one another.

The love that brings couples together can remain untarnished by the accumulation of unresolved arguments that destroy intimacy in marriages and lead caring people into divorce.

Bridges of understanding can begin to span the gulf of hurt feelings that have separated us from the people in our family that we love, but just can't seem to get along with.

Parents can be better models for their children so that future generations can be spared the legacy of unnecessary harsh words and violent behavior.

As we unravel our personal fears, we can begin to collect our reason and bring the factories of ignorance and prejudice to a grinding halt, simply because we no longer participate. We can make the world safer for diversity.

The urge to struggle for power can be replaced with the desire to share power, thereby strengthening our inclination to share our bounty rather than hoard it. A climate of generosity and mutual empowerment will be the forecast for the day.

The stranglehold of power struggle will have loosened its grip on our imaginations, and we can act more collaboratively, dedicating our resources to creation rather than destruction.

As we act more cooperatively and less defensively we can tap into a new wellspring of creativity. New inventions, processes, and systems will emerge that can make a better life for everyone.

More than likely, the fullness of this vision will not manifest in your lifetime. The world as a whole has a lot of evolving to do. But what about your world, the people in your family, at your work, in your neighborhood?

What if, out of your personal commitment to enlightened conflict resolution, you could be the catalyst for a ripple effect going out into your community? Imagine what new possibilities could open up for so many people because of you deciding to make a change in your life and the way you resolve conflict.

You could be the catalyst for a ripple effect going out into your community.

Most of us do not see how our little lives are so intricately woven into the tapestry that is humankind, so we don't recognize our own personal power to contribute to the greater world. But whether your commitment to practice personal responsibility starts a worldwide movement or simply touches all the people you personally meet, we believe the world will be a better place because you were here.

We invite you to join with us in the commitment not to miss one opportunity to transform conflict, confusion, disappointment, or pain into understanding, compassion, wisdom, and goodwill.

About the Authors

Layne and Paul Cutright are authors, speakers, trainers, and coaches who have been professionals in the human potential field since 1976. They have been in a successful romantic and professional partnership for more than twenty-five years.

As a team, they are a force of creative energy, authoring books, courses, and a variety of other educational products. They are innovators in their field, always keeping their eyes on the horizon for new ways to help transform the way people relate.

Both serve on the faculty of Barbara Marx Hubbard's Foundation for Conscious Evolution in Santa Barbara, California, and they are also Directors of Advanced Relationship Coaching with the Relationship Coaching Institute, a virtual university for the professional relationship coach.

Current Projects

The Center for Enlightened Partnership (www.EnlightenedPartners.com)

The Center for Enlightened Partnership is a strategic resource for you in your most important professional and personal relationships. Here they provide their clients with uncommon knowledge, critical distinctions, specific tools, and high-performance, evolutionary practices to ensure extraordinarily rich professional and personal relationships.

At The Center for Enlightened Partnership, you learn the fine art of co-creation so you may design and create partnerships and organizational cultures characterized by creativity, dignity, trust, and heart.

The education available at The Center for Enlightened Partnership is a necessity for anyone who wants to intentionally create a future with someone. Learning how to work together and create environments that foster the evolution of everyone is important because we are all in this together.

You are invited to subscribe to Paul and Layne's free monthly e-zine to receive inspiration, practical tools, tips, and announcements of new programs, services, and products. Go to the website to subscribe.

Paul and Layne's Secrets for Successful Relationships (www.PaulAndLayne.com)

One important measure of the success of your life is the quality of your relationships. For most people, relationships exist as a mystery. They either work out or they don't, without any real understanding of the causes of success or failure. As a result, people often live in their relationships in either a state of hope, resignation, or despair.

At the Secrets website, Paul and Layne focus on romantic and family relationships. The emphasis is less on partnerships and more on the dos and don'ts of simply getting along with people and knowing what you need to work on yourself, for your relationships with others to improve.

If you check out their bookstore, you will discover a variety of e-books, audio programs and other support material available immediately right through your computer.

HeartWired
(www.HeartWired.com)

Long ago, your ancestors gathered around the fire and told stories to help them understand how they fit into the greater scheme of things. The world was far greater than their ability to comprehend it

This is still true for all of us, centuries later.

We are all different, yet we are each important in ways we can't understand until we each share our stories. As we bring our stories to the circle, we begin to connect and build bridges of understanding. We begin to feel our kinship with one another.

At HeartWired, Paul and Layne, with their partner Mark Weaver, help people generate compelling futures around what matters most. They use deep dialog and innovative media to forward the goals of their clients.

HeartWired can help you create a brief, compelling movie that will help you tell a story that deserves and even needs to be told. People create these movies to honor their loved ones and to further the goals in their personal, community, and professional lives.

Let yourself be touched.

Let yourself connect.

Let yourself get HeartWired.

View a variety of movies at the HeartWired website.

Private Intensives and Coaching

Paul and Layne coach individuals, couples, and business partners over the phone and in person. Paul and Layne's favorite coaching work is doing Private Intensives. These custom-designed intensives provide the perfect environment for people in crisis or for people who are ready for an accelerated, breakthrough experience. The use of Relationships Energy Repatterning generates deep and lasting change.

Paul and Layne's work always brings in the added element of a spiritual perspective, so that your accomplishments in the world are in harmony with your hightest values, generating an experience of profound satisfaction with your life.

You may contact Paul and Layne directly by sending an e-mail to partners@EnlightenedPartners.com.

What Others Have to Say About Personal Coaching and Workshops with Paul and Layne

Compassion and Professionalism

"It was my recent privilege to join an entire audience in a standing ovation for Paul and Layne Cutright. Their insights, compassion and professionalism filled everyone with enthusiasm and brought us all to our feet. While they are certain to enhance our abilities to fall in love with each other, it is just as certain that we will fall in love with them. I give them my highest recommendation and urge everyone to enrich their lives with this delightful couple."

—**Gary H. Craig,** Founder of Emotional Freedom Techniques

Highly Effective and Dynamic

"Paul and Layne Cutright are clearly pioneers and leaders in the field of relationship coaching. Their unique blend of personal coaching and energy psychology is highly effective and dynamic. In a very short period of time, using RER, I was able to clear issues I had been struggling with for many years. Thank you!"

—**Karen Curry,** Nurse

Powerful Tools for Daily Life

"Awesome, inspiring, emotional, educational, spiritual, insightful, enlightening, revealing, pivotal and humbling—to say the least. My work with Layne and Paul has been a journey with heart and soul, a healing experience that spans from birth to death to rebirth. I have learned to use some powerful tools in my daily life, I quit my job, which was unfulfilling and uninspiring to me, and I now successfully run my own business. Every aspect of my existence has undergone a powerful evolution to embrace more heart, wisdom and spirit."

—**Mark Herzon,** Computer Reseller

The Right Relationship

"When I came to Paul and Layne, I had lost all hope that I could create the right relationship for me. Now, after only one year, I have met and married the man of my dreams. It would not have been possible without the inner work that I did with Layne and Paul and the curriculum from The Center for Enlightened Partnership. Thank you from the bottom of my heart!"

—**Avonlie Wylson,** Software Executive

Unleashed Creative Energy

"The coaching from Paul has profoundly changed my life. The doubling of my income was only a bonus compared to the unleashing of the creative energy that had been blocked for years. Thank you, Paul!"

—**Larry Gapinski,** Business Owner

Confidence, Well-Being, Peace

"As a business owner and entrepreneur, I was a bit skeptical of coaching at first. But, as I learned to trust the process I ultimately learned to trust my own abilities, which translated into tremendously positive changes in my life both personally and professionally. Personally, I am enjoying more confidence, a greater sense of well-being and peacefulness and better relationships. Professionally, I am better able to size up situations more quickly, I am a better listener and I am better able to inspire cooperation among my employees. I found Paul Cutright to have an uncanny ability to cut through the clutter and get to the essence of what really works!"

—**Sean Curtis,** CEO, Coffee Ambassador

Empowered Rather Than Confused

"Tools like The CURE have helped me to focus on what is going on with me rather than the other person. I now feel empowered rather than confused and defeated after an upset."

—**Ken Courian,** Mechanical Engineer

Potent . . . Unbelievable . . . Incredible

"What a potent combination! My private coaching sessions with Layne complemented and accelerated the class work I was doing at an unbelievable level. This was an incredible gift to myself, and I am grateful every day that I did!"

—**Cary Leone,** Landscape Architect

Safe to Receive Love and Affection

"I have attracted a wonderful man who is helping me to learn that it is truly safe to receive all of his love and affection. I am learning to co-create my partnership with him so I can see, feel and hear all of the things that I desire in our relationship. Most of all, I realize that life is a process and having the tools I learned from Paul and Layne helps me deal with the challenges as they come up."

—**Kathryn Taylor,** Financial Planner

Critical Learning

"I can't believe I wasn't exposed to this material sooner. It is critical learning for anyone who deals with people, anywhere."

—**Ken Abbott,** Engineering Manager

The CURE™ Worksheet
The Conscious Upset Resolution Exercise

Part One, Solo Inquiry (To Do Alone)

Name: _____   **Date:** _____

OBJECTIFY YOUR INTERNAL EXPERIENCE AND VENT

1. **I am feeling:** _____

_____

_____

_____

_____

_____

_____

_____

2. **I am thinking:** _____

_____

_____

_____

_____

_____

_____

_____

_____

BECOME AWARE OF YOUR DRIVING EMOTIONAL FORCES

3. I am upset because: _____

_____

_____

_____

_____

_____

4. My fear in this upset is: _____

_____

_____

_____

_____

5a. How does this upset impact my private and/or public identity?
(How do I think or feel about myself? How might others think or
feel about me because of this situation?) _____

_____

_____

_____

_____

_____

_____

_____

_____

_____

5b. What does it mean about me that . . . ? (Use the reply to question 3 or 4, or both, exactly as written.) _____

_____

_____

_____

_____

_____

_____

_____

_____

_____

_____

_____

_____

_____

6. My bottom-line thought is: _____

_____

_____

_____

_____

WARNING!
DO NOT STOP HERE JUST BECAUSE YOU FEEL RELIEF!

TAKE STEPS TO RESOLVE THE CAUSE OF THE UPSET

7. What resources can I use to heal and resolve my "bottom line" thought (affirmations, belief-change work, energy psychology techniques, other healing/transformational modalities)?

_____

_____

_____

_____

_____

_____

_____

_____

_____

_____

_____

_____

CREATE UNDERSTANDING AND COMPASSION

8. The earliest I can remember feeling this way is: _____

_____

_____

_____

_____

_____

_____

BE RESPONSIBLE FOR YOUR PART AND
CHANGE WHAT DOESN'T WORK

9. The thoughts, feelings, and attitudes I hold that contribute to this current upset are: _____

_____

_____

_____

_____

_____

_____

_____

SEE THE PROBLEM AS A LEARNING/HEALING OPPORTUNITY

10. The learning/growth opportunities for me in this upset are:

_____

_____

_____

_____

_____

_____

_____

_____

_____

_____

_____

_____

CREATE A POSITIVE ACTION PLAN

11. What requests can I make to be responsible for my own needs? How can I turn my complaint into a request and generate cooperation? _____

_____

_____

_____

_____

_____

_____

_____

_____

_____

12. Steps I can take to resolve this current upset are: _____

_____

_____

_____

_____

_____

_____

_____

_____

_____

REWARD AND REINFORCE
THE LEARNING AND HEALING PROCESS

13. How can I/we celebrate this learning experience? _____

_____

_____

_____

_____

_____

Once you have completed Part One, if you are going to engage in the dialogue, Part Two, you'll want to have the guidelines and the illustration handy, so we've provided them again for easy reference.

Guidelines for the Dialogue

1. I will communicate with the intention of producing more harmony and understanding in the relationship.

2. I will participate in a spirit of goodwill, being as honest as I can be.

3. I am committed to a mutually beneficial outcome, recognizing that if one of us loses, the whole relationship loses.

4. I intend to take responsibility for my own experience, knowing it reflects my personal thoughts, beliefs, feelings, and attitudes.

5. I intend to use any mistakes as a learning opportunity, and I will practice a forgiving attitude.

6. I will continue to communicate until we find a resolution that works for everyone involved.

7. I will use the situation to learn about myself and to become a better person.

8. I will keep this conversation confidential and not talk about it with others, unless we both agree otherwise.

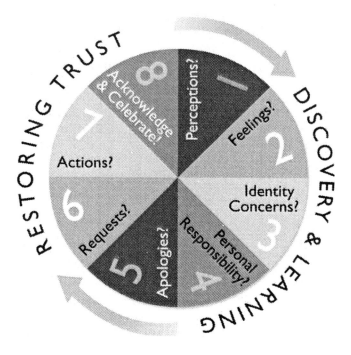

To access this illustration in color, to download the CURE worksheet for use with a computer, or for more information, tools, and resources, please visit the website,

www.EnlightenedPartners.com